ENGAGEMENT
through
DISENGAGEMENT

GAZA and the Potential for Renewed
Israeli-Palestinian Peacemaking

David Makovsky

THE WASHINGTON INSTITUTE FOR NEAR EAST POLICY

© 2005 by the Washington Institute for Near East Policy

Published in 2005 in the United States of America by the Washington Institute for Near East Policy, 1828 L Street NW, Suite 1050, Washington, D.C. 20036.

Library of Congress Cataloging-in-Publication Data

Makovsky, David.
    Engagement through disengagement : Gaza and the potential for renewed Israeli-Palestinian peacemaking / by David Makovsky.
    p. cm.
    ISBN 0-944029-97-3
    1. Arab-Israeli conflict—1993– 2. Israel—Politics and government—1993– 3. Gaza strip—Politics and government—21st century. 4. United States—Foreign relations—Middle East. 5. Middle East—Foreign relations—United States. I. Title.
    DS119.76.M344 2005
    327.7305694'09'0511—dc22

                                                                    2005009351

Design by Daniel Kohan, Sensical Design & Communication
Front cover: AP Wide World Photos/Lefteris Pitarakis

ABOUT THE AUTHOR

DAVID MAKOVSKY IS A SENIOR FELLOW AND DIRECTOR OF THE Project on the Middle East Peace Process at The Washington Institute. He is also an adjunct lecturer of Middle East studies at Johns Hopkins University's Paul H. Nitze School of Advanced International Studies, as well as a member of the Council on Foreign Relations and the International Institute for Strategic Studies.

Author of *A Defensible Fence: Fighting Terror and Enabling a Two-State Solution* (The Washington Institute, 2004) and *Making Peace with the PLO: The Rabin Government's Road to the Oslo Accord* (Westview Press/ HarperCollins with The Washington Institute, 1996), Mr. Makovsky was also a contributor to *Middle East Contemporary Survey* (published by Tel Aviv University's Dayan Center for Middle East Studies) and *Triumph without Victory* (Random House/Times Books, 1992), a retrospective on the 1991 Gulf War. In addition, he has written widely on the Arab-Israeli conflict and the Middle East peace process, with articles appearing in the *New York Times, Washington Post, Los Angeles Times, Wall Street Journal, Financial Times, Foreign Affairs, Foreign Policy,* and *National Interest.* He also appears frequently as a commentator on the *NewsHour with Jim Lehrer* and other leading electronic media.

A former award-winning journalist who covered the peace process for eleven years, Mr. Makovsky served as executive editor of the *Jerusalem Post* and diplomatic correspondent for Israel's leading daily *Haaretz.* In July 1994, with the personal intervention of then–secretary of state Warren Christopher, he became the first journalist writing for an Israeli publication to visit Damascus. That same year, he was a co-recipient of the National Press Club's Edwin M. Hood Award for Diplomatic Correspondence, in recognition of a *U.S. News and World Report* cover story he wrote on Palestine Liberation Organization (PLO) finances.

Mr. Makovsky received a bachelor's degree in history and political science from Columbia University and a master's degree in Middle East studies from Harvard University.

• • •

The opinions expressed in this monograph are those of the author and not necessarily those of the Washington Institute for Near East Policy, its Board of Trustees, or its Board of Advisors.

• • •

TABLE OF CONTENTS

Maps

ACKNOWLEDGMENTS

I WOULD LIKE TO THANK MY RESEARCH ASSISTANT MINDA Lee Arrow for her dedication to this project. She performed a wide array of research tasks, always with unflagging professionalism, a keen sense of detail, and good cheer.

I would also like to thank my colleagues Dennis Ross, Robert Satloff, Michael Herzog, Patrick Clawson, Matthew Levitt, and Michael Eisenstadt, who read various drafts of the paper and were unfailingly generous with their insight and time. I am indebted to others outside The Washington Institute who provided comments on drafts, including Nigel Roberts and Markus Kostner of the World Bank and Larry Garber, who until recently headed the U.S. Agency for International Development mission in the West Bank and Gaza. I would also like to thank those U.S. government officials who offered comments, as well as the 150 people whom I interviewed in Israel, the West Bank, Gaza, Egypt, Jordan, Europe, and, of course, the United States. I am grateful for their ideas, although I alone assume full responsibility for the content of this study.

Shannon Styffe, Michael Bergman, and Ben Fishman were each helpful at different stages of the project, while Anna Hartman deserves special thanks for her work on the maps and appendices. Anna ably assisted me with my previous monograph on the West Bank fence, and I was glad that she could help with this project as well. I would also like to thank Alicia Gansz and George Lopez for seeing the paper through the editorial process.

In addition, I am grateful to the United States Institute of Peace, which invited me to present a paper based on this monograph at a February 2005 Pathways to Peace conference. Exchanging views with colleagues there was an enjoyable experience. Thanks are also due to *Foreign Affairs*, which published an article based on this monograph in its May/June 2005 edition.

Finally, I am indebted to Ellen and Murray Koppelman and Janine and Peter Lowy for their generous support of my work.

FOREWORD

ARIEL SHARON'S DECISION TO WITHDRAW FROM GAZA AND A small part of the West Bank represents a signal development in the Middle East. By withdrawing from all the settlements in Gaza, Israel opens up the possibility of restoring its core bargain with the Palestinian Authority (PA): security for Israelis, freedom for Palestinians. Over the past four-and-a-half years of warfare, both sides came to doubt whether that bargain had any validity. Israelis doubted that Palestinians would ever forsake terrorism in their rejection of the Jewish state, while Palestinians doubted that Israel would ever surrender control over them.

Gaza withdrawal, assuming that it is managed effectively, could address both sets of concerns. Palestinians would see Israel relinquishing control over aspects of their daily lives, and Israelis would see Palestinians assuming their security responsibilities. But the operative words here are "assuming that it is managed effectively."

In this monograph, David Makovsky has done a service by offering a thoughtful analysis of the disengagement, its implications, and the inevitable challenges that must be faced. He explains not just what is at stake in Gaza, but also what issues have to be addressed to ensure success. For example, if Palestinians want Israel to completely withdraw from Gaza, they must help answer security questions related to the smuggling of longer-range ground and surface-to-air missiles along the Philadelphia Route or through a functional Gaza airport or seaport. David's suggestions—including that the Multinational Force and Observers in Sinai play a role on the Egyptian side of the border—are creative and could provide an answer to the smuggling issue.

Similarly, David addresses economic, legal, and political issues that will arise as a result of the withdrawal. In all these sectors, there is no substitute for active coordination between Israelis and Palestinians. Clearly, the disposition of settlement assets—housing, agribusiness, and infrastructure—is particularly important to both peoples. Destruction of these assets would create a terrible symbolic impression at a time when the objective of all parties should be to end the violence and revive a process in which reconciliation once again becomes possible.

As David points out, another top priority will be legitimizing the withdrawal and raising the costs of engaging in violence during or after it. He recommends that the United States work with European and Arab leaders to reject violence generally and, in particular, to discredit any attacks that occur as Israel disengages. After the withdrawal, the UN Security Council could issue a resolution endorsing the Israeli disengagement, recognizing the legal status of the PA in Gaza, and calling for all militias to disband and turn their weapons over to the PA. Such a resolution could create a basis for stability and deter Hamas, Palestinian Islamic Jihad, and other groups from terrorist attacks.

Throughout the monograph, David emphasizes the enormous American stake in the outcome of the disengagement. If carried out smoothly, it will benefit a Palestinian leader—Mahmoud Abbas—who is politically secular, opposes violence, favors reform, and believes in coexistence with Israel. Of course, Abbas must clearly display these attributes in both word and deed. It is equally important that Washington vindicate the Israeli prime minister's decision to withdraw by facilitating a peaceful disengagement that enhances Israeli security and the possibility of partnership.

If there is one relevant lesson to be learned from the past, it is that nothing ever implements itself. David Makovsky has pointed to specific areas in which third-party assistance and facilitation can make the difference between success and failure. Policymakers would be wise to heed his recommendations.

Ambassador Dennis Ross
Former U.S. special Middle East
coordinator for the peace process

EXECUTIVE SUMMARY

RECENT CHANGES IN LEADERSHIP AND POLICY ON THE PAL-
estinian and Israeli fronts have opened a window of opportunity to end
the current violence and return to the peace process. Yasser Arafat's death
paved the way for a more pragmatic Palestinian leadership, and the election of Mahmoud Abbas indicated a recognition on the part of Palestinians that the violence of the intifada must end. As Abbas himself acknowledged, militancy has been politically counterproductive and has failed to
break Israel's will. A return to calm, rather than a continuation of violence,
will make Palestinian aspirations of statehood more feasible.

On the Israeli front, Prime Minister Ariel Sharon's decision to disengage
from the Gaza Strip and the northern West Bank is an important milestone
for both sides. Given Sharon's role as architect of the settlement movement,
he is uniquely positioned to shatter old taboos and, as such, make future
withdrawals more likely. His decision has already helped broaden Israel's
coalition government, providing him with the political backing to carry
out disengagement.

For the Bush administration, the changes provide an opportunity to continue the president's policy of fostering a Palestinian state led by reform-
minded leadership, as he first advocated on June 24, 2002, and repeated in
his 2005 State of the Union address. Moreover, Palestinian elections, like
those in Afghanistan and Iraq, enable the administration to claim success in
the long-term foreign policy goal of democratizing the broader Middle East.
If handled correctly, renewed U.S. involvement would enable Washington to
keep faith with its commitment to ensuring Israel's security, establishing a
Palestinian state, and rebuilding transatlantic alliances.

Indeed, the stakes are high. The future course of the peace process will
be shaped by the disengagement's outcome. If Gaza withdrawal brings
calm, political reform, and a modicum of economic growth, Israelis and
Palestinians will likely press for accelerated peacemaking toward the goal
of conflict resolution. Discussing the endgame before disengagement
would only energize hardline critics and impede dynamics that are critical
to the withdrawal's success. Yet, such discussion need not be ruled out in
the wake of withdrawal.

Alternatively, should Gaza disengagement fail, cynicism and despair are bound to deepen. The violence of the intifada, which has already claimed more than 3,000 Palestinian lives and 1,000 Israeli lives since 2000, would likely swell to its former dimensions, while rejectionists would be emboldened and moderates placed on the defensive.

Reactivating the Roadmap

Although some speculate that Israel's disengagement is meant to supplant the Quartet's Roadmap to Middle East peace, the two initiatives are not at cross purposes. In fact, many of the measures called for in the first phase of the Roadmap are currently being discussed and implemented, including Palestinian elections, security reform, a ceasefire, the halting of incitement, the removal of settlement outposts, and the lifting of checkpoints. Therefore, the United States should look for an opportune moment to announce that the Roadmap has been reactivated and that the Israeli withdrawal will be conducted within its broad context. The Roadmap is the only diplomatic framework generally acceptable to Israelis and Palestinians and backed by the international community. Trust has been shattered between the two sides over the past several years, so resolving the conflict requires a gradual approach focused on two main objectives: providing Israel with security and the Palestinians with a sovereign state.

Security Challenges

The Gaza withdrawal poses numerous security challenges that should be addressed in advance. In theory, the end of Israel's occupation should diminish Palestinian motivations for violence. There are no such guarantees, however. Creative problem solving is needed to curb violence, which could escalate for a variety of reasons, including increased weapons smuggling, chaos in the wake of withdrawal due to lack of law and order, or an energized rejectionist effort spearheaded by Hamas. Any violence directed at Israel could provoke a heavy response, possibly including a return to Gaza. Rejectionist elements may also challenge the Palestinian Authority (PA). In either case, conflict could cripple economic revival in Gaza while simultaneously strengthening those rejectionist groups that, like Hamas, provide essential social services. Continued violence would certainly decrease the chances of the peace process moving forward beyond disengagement.

These concerns affect outside parties as well, given international interest in seeing the peace process resume. Accordingly, the international community will likely assume a role in ensuring that appropriate security measures are taken, all toward facilitating a Gaza withdrawal that enhances the prospects for stabilization. Egypt in particular has a stake in preventing instability, given its shared border with Gaza.

Although Israel's decision to coordinate the pullout with the new Palestinian leadership should encourage ongoing cooperation, the United States must still play a central coordinating role in order to ensure success. Washington took an important step toward this end in February 2005, naming Lt. Gen. William "Kip" Ward to oversee the restructuring of the Palestinian security services. Other tasks for Washington include urging the PA to halt incitement (which the Ward appointment will help address), thereby ensuring that the ceasefire announced at the February 2005 Sharm al-Sheikh summit will become a lasting truce. The United States could also reestablish its Oslo-era trilateral security coordination with Israel and the PA. In order to prevent a cycle of recrimination from emerging, however, Washington will need to be judicious in mediating direct security dialogue between the parties. Bilateral and trilateral security efforts are not mutually exclusive.

A Limited International Dimension

Israel and the PA cannot handle the security challenges posed by Gaza withdrawal on their own. Even with a ceasefire, deep skepticism remains in Israel and abroad about the PA's sustained desire and ability to police Gaza. Indeed, Israel faces an analytical conundrum. The disengagement initiative is popular among Israelis in large part because many of them do not trust the Palestinians. Yet, this very lack of trust leads them to wonder whether the PA will prevent the militarization of Gaza following withdrawal; accordingly, many Israelis have called on the government to maintain control over Gaza's borders even after disengagement. In doing so, however, Israel would not be genuinely disengaging, thereby eliminating any chance that the UN Security Council would endorse the withdrawal. Thus, Israel needs outside help if it is to carry out a disengagement that provides security while releasing it from the need to physically control Gaza.

Defining the precise role of the international community requires careful consideration, however. If the parties have the political will to curb radicalism and violence in Gaza, a multinational force deployed within Gaza could provide the technical capacity to do so. If there is a shortage of political will, however, technical capacity would be of little help; in fact, soldiers from third countries could find themselves in the middle of a dangerous crossfire without a calming strategy. Few countries would deploy their forces under such conditions. Hence, the main problem is one of commitment, not capacity.

Preferably, the international community will take a less dominant, yet no less important, role in helping Israelis and Palestinians confront security challenges. Outside parties could be particularly helpful with three vital tasks: training the PA security services, assisting with security and other arrangements at the Gaza-Egypt border, and creating a mechanism for ongoing consultation on security issues.

Halting the smuggling of arms through tunnels between Egypt and Gaza is an especially critical security challenge. One idea that merits serious consideration is deploying the newly upgraded Egyptian border police force, together with Egyptian intelligence personnel, to the Rafah border area, where they could work alongside a multilateral contingent. This contingent could be part of, or modeled on, the U.S.-led Multinational Force and Observers (MFO) in Sinai, which has helped maintain quiet for much of the quarter-century since the signing of the Egyptian-Israeli peace treaty. U.S. leadership would give the parties confidence, even without a massive infusion of American manpower. (Because the U.S. military is already spread thin, other member countries could contribute additional troops for a Gaza border mission.) The main advantage of operating on the Egyptian side of the border is the area's stability under an established, sovereign government. Moreover, the Palestinian side of Rafah is densely populated, while the Egyptian side has relatively few inhabitants. Operating in Egypt would allow international forces to draw on the expertise of the local border police and other Egyptian security personnel, who know the language and culture and could be most effective in gathering intelligence from the local populace regarding tunnel smuggling.

The mere presence of an MFO at the Gaza border could raise the diplomatic costs to Egypt of not fulfilling its security obligations. At the same time, an MFO could take on a variety of tasks that would ease the burden on the Egyptians, such as monitoring potential infiltration (e.g., at immigration and customs posts at the Rafah terminal), maintaining patrols, and engaging in reconnaissance. A Gaza MFO could also benefit from direct technological assistance by the U.S. Army Corps of Engineers in detecting smuggling tunnels.

Moreover, an MFO could play a role in addressing the formidable security challenges associated with a future Gaza seaport and airport. Multinational troops could eventually help secure such facilities alongside a respected international civilian company specializing in personnel and cargo management, one equipped with the latest in biometric and other technologies. (In the meantime, and perhaps for the long term, the Palestinians could be granted expanded access to outside seaports and airports, which would raise far fewer security risks.)

In order to build confidence and address ongoing security concerns, all parties should discuss the possibility of a consultative mechanism between the Gaza MFO, the PA, Israel, and Egypt. Meetings could be held in the border area shared by the latter three parties, Kerem Shalom.

Economic Viability in Gaza

A variety of measures are needed to foster economic growth in Gaza following Israel's withdrawal:

PA economic reform. All efforts should be put forth to intensify the pace of reform embarked upon by certain PA ministers, including anticorruption measures.

Job creation. Given the uncertain security situation and the logic of disengagement itself, initial efforts to create jobs for Palestinians should not focus on employment in Israel. Apart from security concerns, diversifying employment options within Gaza can help decrease Palestinian economic dependence on Israel. Major infrastructure projects and residential construction in Gaza will be key. As it has done in the past, Israel could provide assurances to third-party donors that, if forced to retaliate for Palestinian attacks, it would not target donor-assisted infrastructure projects. One economic initiative that would entail only minimal security risks is the establishment of Qualified Industrial Zones, which have been successful in Jordan. Industrial parks are a separate issue, given their proven security risks; the two existing parks (the Gaza Industrial Estate at Karni and the Erez Industrial Zone) should be fully utilized before any new parks are built.

Trade facilitation. The Karni passage and other crossing points need to be upgraded, and Israel has indicated that it will take steps toward this end before withdrawal. These efforts, combined with the purchase of additional container scanners and other technology, would provide an adequate security environment and thereby expedite trade from Gaza. Regarding seaborne trade, Israel should consider providing the Palestinians with a pier at the nearby Israeli port of Ashdod, given that a viable Palestinian seaport in Gaza is likely years in the future. Israel is building the final phase of a rail link from Ashdod to Erez (a line from Ashdod to Ashkelon is already in place), which would further facilitate trade. Port Said in Egypt and al-Arish in Sinai could also serve as secure way stations for Palestinian goods.

Standardize procedures at the Karni and Erez terminals. Karni should be kept open whenever possible, with published performance standards and expedited inspection for vendors with proven track records. The Israeli-Palestinian customs union should also be maintained for the time being. Moreover, a secure rail line should be established between Gaza and the West Bank to facilitate the movement of goods. Such a line could become operational once Israel's West Bank fence is completed, thereby minimizing security risks.

Settlements and Housing

Reaching agreement on the highly charged issue of settlement housing may prove particularly difficult. From one perspective, Israeli and Palestinian interests seem to converge: some Israelis wish to destroy settler homes in order to prevent Hamas from flying its flag over them once evacuated, while the PA hopes to replace single-unit housing with multistory buildings, given Gaza's population density. At the same time, Israel fears that media images of such destruction would convince many that Israelis do not want Palestinians to benefit from settlement assets. Given this conundrum, Israel may leave the settlements in place and seek third-party custodianship for them. Because Israelis and Palestinians disagree on the issue of compensation for public infrastructure in the settlements, Israel may find it useful to have a respected international company provide a valuation of such assets. Israel could then present the results during future final-status talks.

Arab Support

In February 2005, the United States committed $350 million in assistance to the Palestinians. Accordingly, Washington should insist that Arab states uphold their pledges of emergency aid made at the 2002 Arab Summit. In fact, they should be urged to increase their support to reflect the windfall they have enjoyed due to increased oil prices in 2003–2004. Persian Gulf states alone have reaped an estimated $100 billion more than their budgetary expectations during this period. After attempting private diplomacy to obtain such support, the United States should not hesitate to go public in order to secure Arab donations.

Arab states could also help revive the multilateral talks of the 1990s, which focused on a variety of largely economic projects with potential benefits for the entire region. Among the topics covered were economic development, water rights, environmental issues, arms control, and refugees. While progress on these issues may vary (with discussion of non-economic issues likely to reap only modest rewards in anticipation of eventual final-status negotiations), such talks would be useful in encouraging regional players to look beyond the territorial issues of the Israeli-Palestinian conflict and consider broader regional change. The mere existence of such negotiations alongside Israeli disengagement would send a message of fresh hope to the peoples of the Middle East.

The Gaza Strip

- Israeli settlements
- Palestinian communities

ELEI SINAI

Erez Crossing

NISANIT

MEDITERRANEAN
SEA

Ash Shati Camp   Jabalya

Gaza City

Salah al-Din Street

Eastern Road

Future site of
Gaza Seaport

NETZARIM

Nahal Oz Crossing

Karni Crossing

Salah al-Din Street

al-Bureij
Camp

KFAR
DAROM

ISRAEL

GUSH
KATIF

N

0   1
mile

Khan Yunis

Gamal Abdul
Nasser Street

MORAG

PHILADELPHIA CORRIDOR

Rafah

Salah al-Din Street

Rafah
Crossing   Sufa Crossing

Gaza Airport
(non-operational)

KEREM
SHALOM

MEDITERRANEAN
SEA

LEBANON   GOLAN
HEIGHTS

Tiberias   SYRIA

Jordan R.

Tel Aviv   WEST
BANK   Amman

Ashdod
Ashkelon   Jerusalem
Gaza City
GAZA   Sderot   Dead
Sea

Port Said

al-Arish   ISRAEL

EGYPT

EGYPT   JORDAN

© 2005 The Washington
Institute for Near East Policy
Source: UN Office for the Coordination
of Humanitarian Affairs

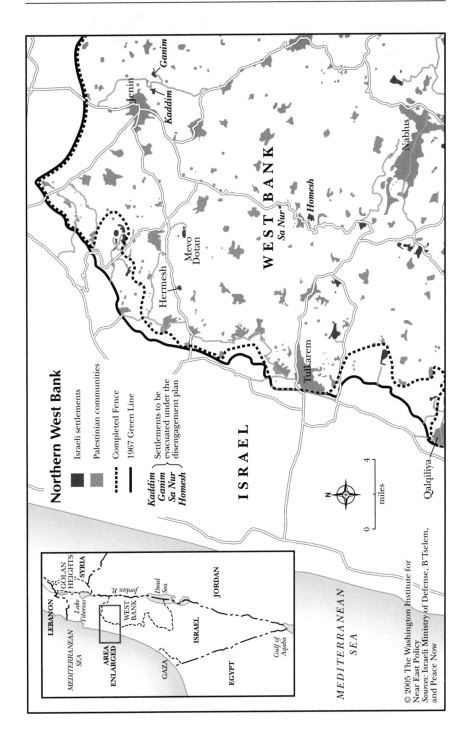

Northern West Bank

- Israeli settlements
- Palestinian communities
- Completed Fence
- 1967 Green Line

Kaddim
Ganim
Sa Nur
Homesh

Settlements to be evacuated under the disengagement plan

ISRAEL

WEST BANK

Jenin
Kaddim
Ganim
Nablus
Homesh
Sa Nur
Mevo Dotan
Hermesh
Tulkarem
Qalqiliya

N

0   4
miles

LEBANON
GOLAN HEIGHTS
SYRIA
MEDITERRANEAN SEA
Lake Tiberias
Jordan R.
WEST BANK
Dead Sea
AREA ENLARGED
ISRAEL
JORDAN
GAZA
EGYPT
Gulf of Aqaba

MEDITERRANEAN SEA

© 2005 The Washington Institute for Near East Policy
Sources: Israeli Ministry of Defense, B'Tselem, and Peace Now

INTRODUCTION

AFTER SEVERAL YEARS OF SUFFERING AND DESPAIR, ISRAELIS
and Palestinians have reason for hope in 2005. Polls indicate greater optimism among both populations than has existed for years, albeit tempered
by cautious realism.[1] Although few in the region believe that violence will
immediately give way to a comprehensive Israeli-Palestinian peace treaty,
many feel that a significantly improved environment is in the offing.

In the wake of Palestinian leader Yasser Arafat's passing in November
2004, a more pragmatic leadership called for elections and pledged to
enact an array of reforms that would hold far-reaching consequences for
Palestinian political development. During the subsequent electoral cam-
paigns, Mahmoud Abbas declared that the "militarization of the intifada"
had been disastrous for the Palestinian people; in winning the presidency,
he received a mandate for such declarations against violence. Meanwhile,
a majority of Palestinians began to oppose suicide attacks in Israel proper
for the first time since the beginning of the intifada in 2000.[2]

These encouraging trends were matched by Israel's decision to withdraw from the Gaza Strip and parts of the northern West Bank. The
disengagement—scheduled to begin in late July 2005—will mark the
first time since 1967 that Israel has evacuated settlements in the territories. Indeed, Prime Minister Ariel Sharon's plan goes well beyond what
is required in the initial phases of the internationally backed Quartet
Roadmap to Middle East peace.

Unlike in the past, Israel will be yielding territory to the Palestinians
outside of a bilateral agreement or defined quid pro quo. Bilateral negotiations have their own obvious rewards, but they are not devoid of problems. In some cases, brinkmanship, poor negotiating dynamics, or other
extraneous factors can derail bilateral initiatives. In other cases, trust is
eroded between parties amid recriminations and infractions. A unilateral
move short-circuits such problems. In the present case, Israel has unilaterally chosen to withdraw from Gaza and the northern West Bank in order
to secure its national interests, making the likelihood of implementation
far higher. One may legitimately question how long Israel can maintain a
unilateral approach, since future territorial issues will be even more sensi-

1

tive. For now, though, it seems to be effective; in fact, Sharon may yield even more under such an approach than he would in a bilateral framework. Moreover, although Sharon has refused to negotiate the fundamental aspects of his disengagement plan, he has made clear his willingness to coordinate its implementation with Abbas. Such cooperation would improve the prospect of postwithdrawal stability.[3]

Disengagement partly reflects the ongoing evolution in Israeli public opinion. It was not long ago that opposition to a Palestinian state was a truism in mainstream Israeli politics. Israelis began to shift away from this position in the 1990s, a trend that intensified more recently as they came to see a two-state solution as the only viable means of ensuring that Israel retains its Jewish, democratic character. That is, if the current demographic situation persists, Jews could find themselves a minority in the combined area of Israel, the West Bank, and Gaza as early as 2010, regardless of their continued majority status in Israel proper. Maintaining control over the territories therefore poses a growing existential threat.

Accordingly, a consistent majority of Israelis support the withdrawal. This change in popular opinion is rooted in a sense of self-confidence rather than defeat.[4] A resilient military and populace, an effective security fence, and the support of the Bush administration all enabled Israel to withstand Palestinian violence, dealing the intifada a major setback, if not an outright defeat. Still, the situation on the ground remains fragile, with the lack of trust between the two peoples profound. Disengagement is therefore a high-stakes affair for all parties.

For Israel, withdrawal represents one of the biggest tests the democracy has faced since its establishment. Even as the disengagement plan passed a variety of parliamentary tests, opposition within his own Likud Party forced Sharon to broaden his government and include the Labor Party. Yet, his ability to navigate the treacherous shoals of Israeli politics has been only half the challenge. Some Israeli religious leaders not only believe that withdrawal constitutes a political miscalculation (i.e., Israel is being duped by Palestinians who in their hearts seek the Jewish state's ultimate destruction), but also assert that no Israeli government has the right to yield biblical patrimony under any circumstances.[5]

Disengagement will also test the new Palestinian leadership, especially if Abbas decides to coordinate the withdrawal with Israel. Failure to accept the Israeli offer of coordination would waste a rare opportunity to renew a much-needed partnership. Yet, Palestinian cooperation must be genuine if it is to help repair the damaged relationship. The more the Palestinian Authority throws its support behind disengagement, the less Abbas will be able to portray it as a unilateral Israeli move.

Regardless of these challenges, the potential benefits of disengagement cannot be overstated. If the withdrawal generates stability and improves the prospects for a better future among Palestinians, it would broaden public support for peace camps in Israel and the territories. Both publics would insist that their respective leaders move forward. A smooth, skillfully coordinated disengagement would also represent a successful test case for revived partnership.

The United States stands to gain much as well. A successful disengagement would enhance America's international and regional standing and permit renewed involvement in Israeli-Palestinian peacemaking. If skillfully handled, such involvement would allow the United States to maintain its commitment to Israeli security, rebuild a frayed transatlantic alliance, and improve ties with the Arab world. A genuine peace process could also help reconcile the contradictory pulls in U.S. Middle East policy: American dependence on affordable Persian Gulf oil, the U.S. presence in Iraq, and the special nature of the U.S.-Israeli relationship.

The consequences of failure or inaction are correspondingly grave, however. If political moderates fail to deliver a better future through disengagement, extremists on both sides will be emboldened, making a resumption of violence likely. An unsuccessful withdrawal would also make it difficult to envision Israelis and Palestinians summoning the requisite will to pursue the Roadmap or move toward final-status negotiations. Moreover, the alternatives to disengagement are all unwise or unworkable. Open-ended Israeli occupation would only lead to growing calls for a "one-state" solution; in light of current demographic trends, such a solution is nothing more than a euphemism for the destruction of Israel and the establishment of "Greater Palestine."

This monograph focuses on Gaza as the most crucial portion of the Israeli disengagement plan. Although the northern West Bank area being evacuated is double the size of Gaza, the latter poses a far sterner test, given its demography, geography, and history. The seaside strip holds nearly 40 percent of all Palestinians living under Israeli control and has long been a bastion for Hamas and other rejectionist factions. Successful disengagement from Gaza would therefore have a disproportionately weighty effect on future peacemaking.

No one should underestimate the challenges ahead. Although both Sharon and Abbas have indicated their willingness to coordinate the pull-out, they face multiple problems in the political, security, and economic spheres. The chapters that follow seek to define those challenges, and to advance ideas for overcoming them in ways that respect Palestinian dignity without harming Israeli security.

Notes

1. According to a poll conducted by the Jerusalem Media and Communications Center in mid-December 2004, 63 percent of Palestinians are optimistic about the future, the highest level since the start of the intifada. Moreover, exit polls conducted by Ramallah-based Bir Zeit University during the January 9, 2005, Palestinian presidential election indicated hopes that Mahmoud Abbas's election would lead to an Israeli withdrawal from Palestinian cities, a resumption of peace talks, and significant Palestinian reforms, including an end to chaos and an improvement in the standard of living. Similarly, a November 28–29, 2004, poll by Tel Aviv University's Tami Steinmetz Center for Peace Research indicated that 70 percent of Israelis are more optimistic than they had been in previous years.

2. Jerusalem Media and Communications Center poll, December 2004.

3. In his December 16, 2004, speech to the Herzliya Conference, an annual forum focusing on Israel's national security challenges, Sharon stated, "In light of the new opportunities and potential of a new Palestinian leadership, Israel will be prepared to coordinate various elements relating to our disengagement plan with the future Palestinian government—a government which is ready and able to take responsibility for the areas which we leave. If this happens, we will have a genuine chance to reach an agreement, and in the future, perhaps also genuine peace. We can reach a situation where terror will stop being such a tangible threat to the well-being of the citizens of Israel. For the first time since the establishment of the state, we will be able to live lives of tranquility, develop and build our economy without disturbance or threat, and invest more in education, health, and welfare. For their part, the Palestinians can then also live in dignity and freedom in an independent state, and, together with us, enjoy good neighborly relations, while cooperating for the good of both our peoples." The full text of the speech is available online (www.pmo.gov.il/nr/exeres/EEDE75B5-9114-4341-80DC-8501F7D3D7F6.htm). See also appendix 1, which contains related passages from Sharon's 2003 Herzliya speech.

4. In his 2004 Herzliya speech, Sharon stated, "Disengagement recognizes the demographic reality on the ground specifically, bravely, and honestly. Of course it is clear to everyone that we will not be in the Gaza Strip in the final agreement. This recognition, that we will not be in Gaza, and that, even now, we have no reason to be there, does not divide the people and is not tearing us apart, as the opposing minority claim. Rather, the opposite is true. Disengagement from Gaza is uniting the people. It is uniting us in distinguishing between goals which deserve to be fought for, since they are truly in our souls—such as

Jerusalem, the large settlement blocs, the security zones, and maintaining Israel's character as a Jewish state—rather than goals where it is clear to all of us that they will not be realized, and that most of the public is not ready, justifiably, to sacrifice so much for. One of the goals of Arab terror was to divide the country and break its spirit. Stopping terror on the one hand, and the disengagement plan on the other, a plan which the great majority of the public supports, forges national unity and creates broad national consensus regarding the justness of our struggle for security, tranquility, and peace."

5. Some sixty religious leaders signed a petition calling on religious soldiers to engage in *siruv pekuda*—that is, to refuse to carry out settlement evacuation orders (Steven Erlanger, "As Gaza Pullout Vote Nears, Tension among Israelis Rises," *New York Times*, October 21, 2004). Moreover, Avi Dichter, head of the Shin Bet, stated that up to 150 settlers are suspected of plotting to assassinate Sharon (Steve Weizman, "Israeli Security Chief Warns, Jewish Settlers Want Sharon Dead," Associated Press, July 20, 2004). Such threats are taken seriously; in 1995, Jewish extremist Yigal Amir killed Prime Minister Yitzhak Rabin six weeks after the Knesset approved the Oslo II agreement.

THE POLITICAL SPHERE: TAKING ADVANTAGE OF OPPORTUNITIES

FELICITOUS CHANGE IN PALESTINIAN LEADERSHIP AT A TIME of bold new Israeli policies has thrown open the proverbial window of opportunity. The coming year promises renewed prospects for movement toward peace, and the United States, more than any other third party, has a vital diplomatic role during this crucial period. Sustained diplomatic engagement that adheres to a well-defined agenda could, relatively quickly, restore trust between the two peoples and reaffirm their faith in the very enterprise of peacemaking.

It is difficult to overstate the importance of the first post-Arafat year and the Israeli withdrawals scheduled to take place during this period. A successful disengagement from Gaza and the northern West Bank would shatter Israeli taboos entrenched since 1967, facilitate additional withdrawals, embolden moderates within each camp, and animate the peace process. Accordingly, all parties should focus first on facilitating the withdrawal—from Gaza in particular—and on helping Palestinian president Mahmoud Abbas maintain calm, curb rejectionists, implement confidence-building measures, and initiate political and security reforms that will improve Palestinians' lives.

The Palestinian Front

When the time came for Yasser Arafat to replace his fatigues with civilian dress, the old warrior balked. He was a committed revolutionary to the end, who never came to grips with the moral legitimacy of Israel's existence or the country's requirements for self-defense. Nor did he believe that the Palestinian polity should develop the democratic and reform-minded institutions needed to cope with the modern world. In 2000, when a final-status deal seemed in the offing at Camp David, Arafat rejected Prime Minister Yitzhak Rabin's offer without making a counteroffer. When the intifada broke out soon afterward, he avoided speaking out against the violence. Only he could have marginalized and shamed those who engaged in such violence, but he pointedly rejected diplomatic entreaties to turn his people away from brutality. Instead, he exhorted them to sacrifice a "million martyrs" in the struggle for Jerusalem. In fact, there are many indications that he himself financed suicide bombings by Fatah's al-Aqsa Martyrs Brigades.[1] Israeli-Palestinian diplomatic relations would never have recovered in his lifetime.

Arafat's leadership was marked by a politics of grievance rather than of governance. He loved the broad strokes of revolutionary tactics but lacked the patience for the bricks and mortar of nation building. The result: a Palestinian Authority (PA) bureaucracy lacking both democratic culture and practice—and swollen with corruption.

Arafat's death in November 2004 allowed pragmatic officials such as Mahmoud Abbas, more competent at administration and institutional governance, to make immediate moves toward mutual accommodation. Arafat's lingering impact on emotional issues such as Palestinian refugees will be more difficult for Abbas to shake, despite his decisive victory in the January 2005 presidential elections. Nevertheless, polling data reveals that Palestinians genuinely yearn for democracy and an end to the conflict. And the election of Abbas signals a political shift away from passion and toward pragmatism—a ballot-box acknowledgment that the violence of the intifada has neither advanced Palestinian national aspirations nor broken Israel's will. Indeed, moving backward over the past four years has perhaps given Palestinians a better perspective on what was right before their eyes in 2000.

The Israeli Front

Prime Minister Ariel Sharon's decision to withdraw from Gaza represents a sea change in Israeli politics. Disengagement will have an immediate effect on the so-called "facts on the ground," given that approximately 1.4 million Palestinians—nearly 40 percent of the population in the occupied territories—live in Gaza. The Israeli plan goes well beyond the requirements of the internationally backed Roadmap. It also marks the first time that Israel has considered evacuating settlements or yielding territory to Palestinian control outside of a bilateral agreement or understanding. Given Sharon's history as the architect of the settlement movement, he is uniquely equipped with both the moral and political authority to launch a process that backs up his repeated calls for "painful concessions" on both sides.

The U.S. Front

President George W. Bush clearly recognizes the diplomatic opportunities created by recent leadership and policy changes in the Israeli-Palestinian arena. He has publicly committed to prioritizing this issue in his second term, comparing it in significance only to his highest-priority domestic policy issue, Social Security reform. Although critics have questioned the sincerity of his stated commitment to Israeli-Palestinian peace, there are several reasons to believe that the president genuinely regards progress on this front as an essential component of his broader Middle East policy goals.

Such progress would fulfill a number of the president's objectives. First, it would be a vindication of the June 24, 2002, speech, in which he rejected Arafat's capacity for leadership and made Palestinian institutional reform a cornerstone of U.S. policy. Indeed, the president emphatically conditioned good U.S.-Palestinian relations on Arafat's departure from leadership. This condition was predicated on Bush's sense that Arafat was not truly committed to coexistence with Israel. Given the promising democratic activity that emerged in the Palestinian sphere following Arafat's death—the January presidential elections, upcoming legislative elections in July, and the staggered municipal elections that began in December 2004—Bush can confidently reiterate the importance of U.S. diplomatic engagement with the Palestinians. He can also reassert U.S. diplomatic leadership to ensure that the first steps taken by Israel and the reformed Palestinian leadership put the peace process back on track, highlighted by withdrawal from Gaza.

Second, the president can characterize Palestinian elections as a successful component of his broader democratization agenda in the region, alongside elections in Afghanistan and Iraq. Yet, it is crucial that Palestinian elections be perceived not as a product of American diktat, but as a consequence of the profound desire among Palestinians for democratic expression.

Third, advancing the cause of Israeli-Palestinian peace enables the United States to maintain its commitment to Israel's perpetual security. By firmly rejecting authoritarian and violent impulses among the Palestinian leadership while nurturing democratic and pragmatic reform, Washington can demonstrate to the Israelis that their security remains a paramount consideration. Such a stance would also show the Palestinians that U.S. allegiance to the cause of Israeli security does not necessarily jeopardize their own national aspirations.

Fourth, committed American involvement in Israeli-Palestinian diplomacy can improve ties between the United States and its European allies. Much of the groundwork for an improved transatlantic relationship has already been laid. President Bush declared that he would invest the "capital of the United States" to the cause of peace at a joint press conference alongside visiting British prime minister Tony Blair (see appendix 2 for relevant excerpts from the press conference).[2] Blair withstood heavy domestic criticism for his role as the key U.S. ally in Iraq, and he now feels well positioned to bring European influence to bear on Israeli-Palestinian negotiations. In general, Europe has resolutely focused on the Palestinian cause even as U.S. attention was diverted to Iraq and the broader war on terror. Increased U.S. diplomatic attention will remind and reassure European allies that the United States shares their desire for a just settlement.

The president reinforced this notion through two other steps. In his January 2005 State of the Union address, he announced that the United States would deliver $350 million in aid to the Palestinians. This commitment was reiterated when Secretary of State Condoleezza Rice attended the Palestinian reform conference in London in March. Rice also announced that the United States would dispatch Army general William "Kip" Ward to help restructure the PA security services and revive Israeli-Palestinian security cooperation.

The manifold benefits of U.S. diplomatic engagement are clear. Moreover, there is good reason to believe that U.S. influence on the Israeli-Palestinian issue can be particularly effective during this administration. Not since President George H. W. Bush and his confidant and trusted advisor James Baker has there been such an intimate relationship between a president and his secretary of state. Unlike her predecessors Warren Christopher, Madeleine Albright, and Colin Powell, Rice will speak with the total confidence and authority of the president. The well-known intimacy between the two will bolster American influence whenever foreign leaders consider the degree to which the secretary of state is empowered to act on behalf of the administration.

The Perils of an All-or-Nothing Approach

Although optimism is warranted, the auspicious conditions for diplomatic progress should not give way to expectations of immediate resolution of this decades-long conflict. Breakthroughs are possible, but they will not happen at breakneck speed. However one evaluates Arafat's legacy, his shadow will loom large at least in the near term. His public calls for Palestinian "martyrs"—exhortations that glorified suicide bombers and strengthened radicalism in general—will not soon fade from the popular Palestinian memory. Neither will the severely damaged trust between Israelis and Palestinians be quick to heal.

Moreover, Arafat's unyielding position on the refugee question—namely, that Palestinian refugees be permitted to resettle in Israel in addition to a future Palestinian state—created a diplomatic chasm that will not be easily bridged. For Arafat, both this position and that of exclusive Palestinian sovereignty over contested religious sites in Jerusalem were part of the Palestinian self-definition. Although decisive Palestinian elections provided Abbas with the legitimacy to speak on his people's behalf, there is scant evidence to suggest that he will resist pressure from Palestinians on these most controversial and emotional issues. After four-and-a-half years of terror and violence, Israeli politicians are similarly unwilling to make the necessary sacrifices on sensitive issues such as Jerusalem. In fact, raising these issues prematurely threatens the favorable short-term political dynamics, particularly regarding the Gaza withdrawal.

Given these temporarily intractable issues, an all-or-nothing diplomatic orientation toward peacemaking—a mandate to resolve the conflict entirely or fail trying—will only ensure an undesirable or unrealistic outcome. There is an attractive middle course, however. Diplomatic engagement on a more circumscribed agenda, with the goal of restoring trust and reaffirming both people's faith in the peacemaking process, can open a path to eventual final-status negotiations. As mentioned previously, the first post-Arafat year should be focused on restoring calm in volatile areas, implementing mutual confidence-building measures, and enabling an orderly Israeli exit from Gaza. Successful execution of these goals would do much to restore trust, and would augur well for a historic and lasting reconciliation. Accordingly, the bulk of this study focuses on this initial period, particularly the Gaza withdrawal, examining which diplomatic policies will maximize the prospects of success—and minimize the terrible danger of lost opportunity.

Withdrawal Can Complement the Roadmap

One fundamental question presents itself from the outset: does Israel's "Gaza First" plan represent a departure from the internationally backed Roadmap, or will it facilitate implementation of that plan? On June 24, 2002, President Bush outlined his vision of a two-state solution to the Israeli-Palestinian conflict. The Roadmap is a set of markers intended to light the way to that vision, as endorsed by the international community. (See appendix 3 for the full text of the Roadmap. Also see appendices 4 and 5 for related statements by the Quartet and the G-8.) It has both advantages and disadvantages. Its chief disadvantage, obviously, is that the affected parties themselves did not author it. Consequently, they lack a sense of ownership over the process and may not adhere to every sentence within it as rigorously as the outlined sequence dictates. The document must therefore be somewhat flexible, able to cope with an evolving situation.

But the advantages of the Roadmap are undeniable. It is the only diplomatic framework broadly acceptable to both parties and backed by the international community. It acknowledges the shattered trust between Israelis and Palestinians and makes clear that resolution of the conflict must be rooted in gradual steps. It has a clearly defined objective: an end to Israeli occupation of Palestinian territory—while ensuring Israeli security—through the implementation of a two-state solution. Moreover, although it includes a rough timetable, progress through its three phases requires mutual performance. In this sense, it builds on UN Security Council Resolution 242, which enshrined the land-for-peace concept of fairness in mutuality: neither side can be the sole beneficiary.

The Roadmap has come under legitimate criticism in the past. When it was unveiled in spring 2003, neither the Palestinians nor the Israelis made meaningful attempts to implement the first phase. Critics also questioned U.S. commitment, suggesting that the chief purpose of the diplomatic blueprint was to assuage European and Arab concerns about the looming Iraq war. Despite these criticisms, policy and leadership changes in the region justify the Roadmap's renewed prominence.

Similarly, many of the critics who claim that Sharon is yielding Gaza only as a ruse to preserve Israel's hold on the West Bank are the same individuals who failed to predict the sea change itself: Israel's unilateral disengagement. For the architect of the settlements to himself break the taboo of evacuation makes it more likely that Gaza withdrawal will facilitate rather than impede similar moves in the West Bank. Moreover, the route of Israel's West Bank security fence—which, as of February 2005, is slated to include as little as 8 percent of West Bank land on the Israeli side of the barrier—is an implicit acknowledgment that Israel does not intend to exercise permanent control over the vast majority of that territory.[3] In this sense, the disengagement plan complements the broad goals of the Roadmap.

Indeed, Phase I of the Roadmap is already being implemented: the Palestinians have held an election, and Abbas has publicly committed, and already begun, to reform the PA and restructure its security services. Just days after being elected, Abbas stated, "There are mutual obligations in the Roadmap and we're serious about starting to implement our obligations immediately."[4] Moreover, by declaring his dedication to the Roadmap in Arabic to his own people, he gave a significant indicator of his sincerity and determination.[5] Sharon has also made several statements suggesting that the Roadmap is the only diplomatic plan acceptable to Israel—in fact, the willingness of both leaders to declare their commitment to the plan is one of the key reasons why the diplomatic community should energetically support it.

Despite being assuaged somewhat by the Palestinians' initial steps, Israel will demand concrete counterterrorism measures—required by the Roadmap—as a prerequisite to future phases. The first phase also requires elimination of incitement to violence. The new Palestinian leadership has taken some preliminary steps in this regard, steps it can reinforce by periodically reviewing its educational curriculum and removing imams who deliver incendiary sermons. For its part, Israel should honor its Roadmap commitment to remove unauthorized settler outposts and curb settlement activity. By ensuring that these steps are carried out successfully, the United States will be able to highlight its continued commitment to a performance-based approach and preserve the balance inherent in that strategy.

In the short term, a number of scheduled actions—some officially noted, others not—suggest that the two parties are indeed deep in the process of implementing the Roadmap's first phase. The following sections discuss the details of several such initiatives.

Palestinian Institution Building

The Roadmap places a premium on Palestinian democratization—a frequent theme for President Bush ever since his June 24, 2002, speech, one recently reinforced in his joint press conference with Tony Blair in November 2004. Perhaps because of its emphasis in the Roadmap, the encouragement of robust Palestinian democracy is incorrectly perceived by some as an external imposition of American or Western values. In fact, this facet of the Roadmap echoes a desire for democracy that is deeply felt on the Palestinian street. According to a poll conducted in September 2004, only 29 percent of Palestinians were satisfied with the state of Palestinian democracy at the time.[6] Calls for democratization have occupied a central plank in the platform of the Fatah young guard, who saw Arafat's authoritarian style as responsible for rampant corruption among the old guard.

The Roadmap calls on the Palestinians to "hold free, open, and fair" elections "as early as possible," and "in the context of open debate and transparent candidate selection/electoral campaign based on a free, multiparty process." When the PA held presidential elections on January 9, 2005, it did so not just in response to the Roadmap, but also in conformity with the Palestinian Basic Law, which required that presidential elections be held within sixty days of Arafat's death. By fall 2004, the Palestinian Central Elections Commission (CEC) had registered 67 percent of all eligible voters in the first registration drive since the previous Palestinian elections in 1996, which involved 1.1 million Palestinian voters from the West Bank and Gaza.[7] The CEC estimated voter turnout on election day at 71 percent. Municipal elections—the first since 1976—began in December 2004 and will follow a staggered schedule during 2005. As of March 2005, these elections have been running smoothly. Elections for the Palestinian Legislative Council are scheduled for July 17, 2005.

Another component of Palestinian elections—balloting for the Fatah Party—is also tentatively scheduled for June 2005. Historically, Fatah was the mainstream branch of the Palestinian national movement. Yet, Arafat's increasingly authoritarian leadership style caused his party to ossify, breeding cronyism and corruption among an entrenched ruling class. One consequence of this paralyzed leadership was the growth of Hamas, which attracted increasing numbers of ordinary Palestinians by cultivating a reputation for lack of corruption. Now Hamas has made clear that it will compete in both the legislative and municipal elections. The group's success in sweeping local Gaza elections in January 2005 was a cautionary note: if Fatah is to field strong competitors against Hamas, it must find candidates who are not mired in corruption. The Fatah young guard recognize the need to return the party to its former status as politically dynamic and attuned to the social needs of the public. They see Fatah democratization as essential for future Palestinian political development and as a key means of cleansing the party of old guard corruption and cronyism.

Incitement

The Roadmap requires that, at the very outset of Phase I, "All official Palestinian institutions end incitement against Israel." Since Arafat's death, Sharon has indicated that this step is a priority, even more so than Israeli demands that Palestinians crack down on rejectionist groups. According to Radwan Abu Ayash, head of the Palestinian Broadcasting Company, Abbas himself took action on this front in November 2004, ordering official Palestinian media to avoid broadcasting anything that could be interpreted as incitement.[8] Such a step, while preliminary, is promising.

Security Reform

In his final years, Arafat came under increasing international pressure to reform and unify his security services. Calls for security reform came from CIA director George Tenet (in 2001), U.S. envoy Gen. Anthony Zinni (2002), the text of the Roadmap (2003), and Egyptian intelligence chief Omar Suleiman (2004). Such demands were issued not only by foreigners, but also by the Palestinian legislature in summer 2002. Of course, no serious reforms were undertaken, though Arafat or one of his top aides promised change each time.

Genuine reform of the Palestinian security services is critical both in Gaza and the West Bank. Without it, hope for stability and economic growth is seriously impaired. Abbas seems willing to implement meaningful security reforms, but he will need help.

Such reform is in the Palestinians' own interest, as Abbas acknowledged when he stated, "We have to take care of security—not for the sake of the Israelis but for the sake of the Palestinians."[9] When asked explicitly about unifying the security forces, he replied, "We will unify [them] and transfer the authority [over them] to the prime minister, according to the road map."

Salam Fayad, a veteran International Monetary Fund official who was appointed Palestinian finance minister amid heavy international pressure on Arafat, will play a key role in this effort. Fayad took steps toward increased financial transparency even in the face of Arafat's obstructionism. Now he must ensure that the PA's security organizations are adequately and properly funded. The PA took a first step in this regard in spring 2004, after the European Union threatened to withhold funding if financial reforms were not implemented. Arafat eventually capitulated, allowing security officials to open bank accounts and receive monthly salaries. Previously, Arafat had disbursed large amounts of cash directly to security chiefs, who then paid their subordinates, a practice that encouraged and enabled massive corruption. Fayad's reformist tendencies suggest he might attempt to augment these preliminary reforms by instituting an oversight mechanism that enables funding for security organizations to be deposited directly into the bank accounts of security officials.

Reform is only a first step, however; security services require training. Egypt has begun training Gaza security officials in advance of the Israeli withdrawal, and similar offers have been extended by several Arab and European states. The United States should resume its own training of Palestinian security officials, begun in the mid-1990s as a counterterrorism measure. To help facilitate the Roadmap, Washington should also consider resuming its role as security liaison between Israeli and Palestinian officials. For the immediate future, though, it may be more useful to maintain separate bilateral talks, with the goal of resuming trilateral talks after confidence has been rebuilt. These issues will be discussed in greater depth in chapter 3.

Ceasefire

Phase I of the Roadmap calls on the Palestinian leadership to issue an "unequivocal statement reiterating Israel's right to exist in peace and security and calling for immediate and unconditional ceasefire to end armed activity and all acts of violence against Israelis anywhere." Abbas has pledged to obtain a ceasefire from the various Palestinian factions,[10] and Israel has indicated it would respect such a cessation of hostilities (as mentioned above, chapter 3 elaborates on this and related security issues).

Settlements

Israel's obligations under the first phase of the Roadmap include the following forward-looking stipulation: "As comprehensive security performance moves forward, IDF [Israeli Defense Forces] withdraws progressively from areas occupied since September 28, 2000, and the two sides restore the status quo that existed prior to [then]. Palestinian security forces redeploy to areas vacated by IDF." In a December 2004 speech, Israeli foreign minister Silvan Shalom acknowledged Israel's obligation to withdraw to the September 28 lines as Palestinian security capabilities improve. This issue was central to Defense Minister Shaul Mofaz's conversations with top PA security officials in the aftermath of Abbas's election victory. Improvement in Palestinian security will also have a salutary effect on the number of Israeli roadblocks in the West Bank. Before the intifada erupted in 2000, few such roadblocks existed; as the intifada ebbs and Israel relies on its security fence to prevent infiltration, the need for roadblocks will once again be minimized. Indeed, according to senior Israeli security officials, the number of roadblocks had already been halved by early 2005 due to decreasing violence and the fence's success in halting attacks.[11]

In accordance with the Roadmap, Israel will be asked to make good on its public commitment to dismantle settler outposts established since March 2001. The government has taken down some, but not all, such outposts. The Roadmap also calls for a freeze on construction in established settlements. This requirement is expected to meet with greater resistance. While rejecting any moral equivalence between terrorist groups and settlers, Israel will assert that it is unfair to demand the freezing of all settlement growth at a time when the Palestinians refuse to crack down on their own rejectionists—particularly when Israel is going above and beyond Roadmap requirements by dismantling, not merely freezing, all established settlements in Gaza and parts of the northern West Bank. In an April 14, 2004, letter to then–national security advisor Condoleezza Rice, Sharon's top aide Dov Weisglass stated that Israel would limit settlement expansion to already built-up areas and not expropriate any new land.

Why has it been so difficult for Israel to restrain settlement activity and dismantle illegal outposts? The obstacles are judicial, organizational, and political. Settlers have been quite adroit in finding judicial loopholes that enable them to avoid compliance with orders to dismantle outposts. For example, they will move or rearrange the mobile caravans that constitute most outposts and then claim that a given evacuation order applies only to the previous configuration of temporary structures. Other settlers have persuaded the courts that they should not be bound by demarcation agreements if they freely purchased the land in question. Sharon himself is responsible for some of the organizational barriers that hinder settlement reform. In early 2004, he and Defense Minister Mofaz tasked retired army general Baruch Spiegel with monitoring illegal settlement activity.

Yet, this move came only belatedly, spurred by U.S. concerns, and Spiegel was given a relatively small staff of ten.[12] Sharon also tasked a lawyer, Talia Sasson, with investigating government complicity in outpost activity. In February 2005, she issued a scathing report asserting that the government was indeed involved in funding outposts.[13]

These legal and organizational difficulties have enhanced a formidable political obstacle—namely, regional suspicions about Sharon's ultimate intentions regarding West Bank settlements. Sharon's failure to dismantle settlement outposts has led to rare but real friction between the prime minister and President Bush. What is required, therefore, is political will, including legislation that closes loopholes on the outpost issue and prevents its further exploitation by settlers. Moreover, Israel should take greater pains to enforce—through all available administrative means—proper lines of demarcation for "natural growth" of built-up settlements.

Gaza Coordination

Israeli withdrawal from Gaza can be either chaotic or orderly. Obviously, the prospects for long-term peace will be enormously improved by a smooth handover, and both sides—as well as the international community—have a vested interest in a calm and organized transfer of responsibility. Without careful planning and coordination, however, chaos is likely.

Handled properly, the withdrawal will help stabilize Gaza, which has long been riddled by violence and poverty, and thus expedite the peace process. Conversely, a chaotic handover will revive Israeli memories of the messy exit from Lebanon in 2000, to which some Israelis attribute the growth of Palestinian militarism. Indeed, a chaotic withdrawal could strengthen the hand of Palestinian rejectionist groups such as Hamas. These groups hope to depict the Gaza pullout as a forced retreat under fire, as Hizballah did with the Lebanon withdrawal. Such an impression would vindicate Hamas's militant approach and burnish the organization's standing in the aftermath of the withdrawal.

Sharon has made clear that Israel will not allow itself to be seen as retreating under fire and will not hesitate to fire back, out of both self-defense and a desire to protect its national prestige. Israel's determination to answer fire with fire was on display in late summer and fall 2004, when it responded to Qassam rocket attacks against the border town of Sderot (a few miles from Sharon's private home) by attacking northern Gaza in an effort to push militants out of range. Such incidents have already created an escalatory dynamic.

The Role of Outside Actors

A sincere return to the Roadmap and a smooth Gaza handover will require the careful coordination of many players with manifold agendas. Accordingly, the United States must be a diplomat among diplomats, able to predict and coordinate the future steps of the other principal actors: Israel, the PA, Egypt, and the other three branches of the Quartet (the UN, the European Union, and Russia). American involvement can be particularly effective in demonstrating to the beleaguered Palestinian people the clear advantages of peaceful reconciliation over violent uprising (e.g., economic incentives). Overall, Washington should keep its immediate focus on disengagement, ensuring that the parties do not misinterpret each other and coordinating the actions of myriad players.[14]

The political road ahead will require careful navigation by the United States, given that neither the Palestinians nor the Israelis are ready for final-status talks. Still, real progress is possible, and committed U.S. involvement would help both sides see the light at the end of the tunnel. By formally activating the first phase of the Roadmap, Washington would signal that U.S. endorsement of Gaza withdrawal is part of a long-term strategy. Such a diplomatic posture would bolster Abbas's reputation—particularly among Palestinians—as a leader able to secure U.S. involvement in a wider process, so that "Gaza First" does not become "Gaza Only." It would also reassure Israel of Washington's commitment to a performance-based approach. More than any other factor, Israel views the Palestinian counterterrorism efforts mandated by Phase I of the Roadmap as a prerequisite to implementation of future phases.

As for Egyptian involvement, Cairo, like the other principal players, has a keen interest in a successful handover of authority in Gaza. In recent years, Egypt has contented itself with merely perfunctory efforts to discover and block the many arms-smuggling tunnels that dot its border with Gaza. Egypt's laxity in this regard is attributable not only to the economic benefits that families on both sides of the Rafah border reap from smuggling, but also to Cairo's longstanding hope that Israel would assume primary responsibility for policing the tunnels.

With Israel's exit in sight, however, Egypt's attitude has changed. In December 2004, for example, Cairo committed to upgrading its border police contingent stationed in Sinai adjacent to southern Gaza. The enhanced and expanded force is scheduled for deployment in summer 2005 in advance of Israel's withdrawal. The border guards will reportedly be supplemented by an unspecified number of Egyptian intelligence officers, who can glean information about any ongoing smuggling from the Sinai border populace.

Having battled its own Islamist militants throughout the 1990s, Egypt is deeply concerned about the threat of a Hamas takeover in Gaza. Egyptian security officials have privately stated, "We cannot permit a Muslim Brotherhood state on our eastern frontier."[15] Still, it is unrealistic to believe that Egypt will take ultimate responsibility for Gaza's stability following the Israeli pullout. Cairo has no desire to be seen, at home or abroad, as opposing Palestinian nationalism or, worse, becoming the new "occupier" of Gaza. Hence, Egypt's role in the withdrawal, while important, will necessarily be limited in scope; Gaza will not return to its pre-1967 status as a de facto Egyptian province. The specifics of Egypt's proper security role will be discussed in chapter 3.

UN Resolution

Assuming Israel does in fact carry out a comprehensive withdrawal from Gaza, the UN Security Council should pass a resolution certifying the disengagement as soon as possible thereafter. Such a resolution would have several benefits. For Israelis and Palestinians, it could reinforce a sense of calm and codify security arrangements coordinated by the parties in advance of the pullout. A resolution would also be a valuable incentive for those seeking to ensure that Israel does not remain on the so-called Philadelphia Road (the narrow corridor between Egypt and Gaza) indefinitely. Without such a resolution, Israel is more likely to maintain a presence in the corridor.

In order to make full use of the international community's power to delegitimize violence and codify prewithdrawal security arrangements, any postwithdrawal resolution should demand that all Palestinian militias disband and submit their weapons to the PA. Although skepticism is certainly warranted regarding the likelihood of militant compliance with such a demand, the international community must nevertheless go on record asserting that these groups lack any shred of legitimacy. Moreover, in the interest of encouraging future Israeli withdrawals, the Council should formally acknowledge that Resolutions 242 and 338 have been fulfilled with regard to Gaza once Israel completes its disengagement.

A new resolution could be particularly useful in assuring outside parties that the pullback is complete. After all, it is the Security Council that provided an international imprimatur to the Israeli withdrawal from Lebanon in 2000, removing a crucial item from the list of Arab grievances against Israel. That resolution has undoubtedly contributed to the relative quiet since then along the Lebanon-Israel border, despite the previously mentioned negative aspects of the withdrawal (i.e., increased Palestinian militarism and an emboldened Hizballah).

Israel would no doubt regard this proposal with skepticism, fearing that the UN would seek to hijack the process by setting the standard for certification unacceptably high. As such, it would likely prefer to short-circuit the Security Council idea entirely. Yet, the United States could quietly consult with the Council's five permanent members about the viability of a resolution in advance of it being brought to the floor. If support were insufficient, the resolution could always be withdrawn before reaching a vote.

Notes

1. Matthew Levitt, *Targeting Terror: U.S. Policy toward Middle Eastern State Sponsors and Terrorist Organizations, Post–September 11* (Washington, D.C.: The Washington Institute for Near East Policy, 2002), pp. 26–27.

2. "President and Prime Minister Blair Discussed Iraq, Middle East," transcript of White House press conference, Washington, D.C., November 12, 2004. Available online (www.whitehouse.gov/news/releases/2004/11/20041112-5.html).

3. David Makovsky and Anna Hartman, "Israel's Newly Approved Security Fence Route: Geography and Demography," PeaceWatch no. 495 (March 3, 2005). Available online (www.washingtoninstitute.org/templateC05.php?CID=2268). The article includes a map of the revised route.

4. Diala Saadeh, "Abbas Says Palestinians to Move on Roadmap," Reuters, January 13, 2005.

5. Mahmoud Abbas, interview, Voice of Palestine Radio, January 25, 2005. When asked about an upcoming meeting with Sharon, Abbas replied, "[T]he issues we will raise are the current issues that have to do with the implementation of the Roadmap, the first part of the Roadmap. Then we will definitely discuss withdrawal from Gaza."

6. Khalil Shikaki, "Public Opinion Poll #13: Results," Palestinian Center for Policy and Survey Research, September 23–26, 2004. Available online (www.pcpsr.org/survey/polls/2004/p13a.html).

7. Palestinian Central Elections Commission, "46% of Registered Voters are Youths, 46% are Women," November 23, 2004. Available online (www.elections.ps/english/news/details.php?id=255).

8. Muhammad Daragahmeh, "In Gesture, Palestinian Leader Orders Media to Stop Anti-Israel Incitement," Associated Press, November 30, 2004. Ayash stated, "Abu Mazen [Mahmoud Abbas] asked us to be sure that the material we broadcast does not contain any material that could be considered incitement."

9. "Q&A: Another Chance," *Washington Post*, November 28, 2004.

10. Ibid. Abbas stated, "I started a dialogue with Hamas, PIJ (Palestinian Islamic Jihad), and the Al-Aqsa Martyrs Brigade. I cannot say that we have reached an agreement. Our goal is to cool down the whole situation, to stop all kinds of violence and terror."

11. In a January 31, 2005, interview with the author, Baruch Spiegel, Mofaz's advisor for humanitarian affairs, insisted that the number of remaining roadblocks was a fraction of the figure claimed by different nongovernmental groups.

12. The inadequate staff size becomes clear when one considers the formidable tasks assigned to Spiegel. In addition to monitoring outpost activity, he was charged with demarcating the boundaries of each and every West Bank settlement. This assignment stemmed from Israel's commitment (made at the June 2003 Aqaba summit) to provide the United States with a yardstick for determining whether settlement expansion was indeed occurring. He was also designated the point man for resolving humanitarian problems arising from construction of the West Bank fence.

13. See Talia Sasson, "Summary of the Opinion Concerning Unauthorized Outposts," Israeli Ministry of Foreign Affairs, March 10, 2005. Available online (www.mfa.gov.il/NR/rdonlyres/5AD2CBB2-851D-4917-89B2-CFF60C83C16C/0/SummaryoftheOpinionConcerningUnauthorizedOutposts.doc).

14. At a conference held by the U.S. Institute of Peace on January 27, 2005, Professor Steve Spiegel (a longtime Israeli-Palestinian observer from UCLA) suggested the creation of a special "Office of Disengagement Management" for this purpose.

15. Information obtained from author interviews with senior Egyptian military officials in Cairo (April 2004) and Washington (July and October 2004).

LEGAL IMPLICATIONS
OF WITHDRAWAL

ANY DISCUSSION OF GAZA'S FUTURE LEGAL STATUS MUST BEGIN
with an examination of its status during the past century. In the aftermath
of World War I, the area was placed under the British Mandate. Following
World War II, it was mentioned in the Egyptian-Israeli General Armistice
Agreement of February 24, 1949, which delineated its territorial boundaries (in Article VI) but did not clarify its legal status. In practice, Egypt
occupied Gaza between the 1948 establishment of the state of Israel and
1967, although it did not formally annex the territory.[1]

During those years, Gaza witnessed frequent conflict. Although Egypt
formally decried aggression against Israel, Egyptian-backed *fedayeen* used
the Strip as a launching pad for attacks, which in turn led to Israeli reprisals into Gaza.[2] Israel seized both Sinai and Gaza during the Suez Canal
War in 1956, but yielded to U.S. pressure and relinquished both territories
in March 1957, with the understanding that Sinai would go to Egypt and
Gaza would be turned over to the UN Emergency Force (UNEF).[3] Several days after the Israeli withdrawal, however, Egyptian president Gamal
Abdul Nasser declared that Gaza would be placed under Egyptian administrative control, though he permitted UNEF to remain in place.[4] The UN
subsequently moved its forces to the Gaza perimeter.

During the 1967 war—triggered in large part by Nasser's expulsion of
UNEF from Sinai[5]—Israel reoccupied both Sinai and Gaza. The resulting
UN Security Council Resolution 242 called on Israel to withdraw from
areas it conquered during the war in return for peace, without specify-
ing what legal status would be accorded to these territories. Consequently,
Gaza's legal status has been a subject of negotiation in all post-1967 peace
conferences and agreements, including the 1991 Madrid conference, the
1993 Oslo Accords, UN Security Council Resolution 1397 of 2002 (which
called for a two-state solution), and the 2003 Roadmap.

It is worth noting that Gaza and the West Bank city of Jericho were the
first areas made subject to the 1993 Oslo Declaration of Principles, with
the formal Gaza-Jericho agreement signed in Cairo in May 1994. Jericho
was added to the deal primarily to allay Palestinian fears that the interim
agreement would only affect Gaza. Israel's current plan to evacuate four

settlements in the northern West Bank alongside its wholesale withdrawal from Gaza was crafted with the same idea in mind.

Defining Israeli, Palestinian, and International Interests

Should Gaza be declared a Palestinian state following the Israeli withdrawal? Clearly, the pullout is an opportunity to replace the territory's 100-year history of legal ambiguity with a stable and clearly defined status acceptable to all interested parties. First, however, the interests of those parties must themselves be defined.

Israeli interests. Israel wants its withdrawal to signify both a de facto and a de jure end to its responsibility for the welfare of Gaza's population.[6] The Israeli occupation has garnered wide international criticism and is perceived as a motivator of suicide bombings, rocket attacks, and other hostilities. Clearly, then, it is in Israel's interest to carry out a withdrawal that is internationally recognized as terminating all Israeli legal responsibility for the territory and its residents.

Territorial disengagement is also part of Israel's strategy to ward off a demographic threat to its national identity. Currently, an estimated 51 to 54 percent of the combined population of Israel, the West Bank, and Gaza is Jewish. Yet, if the status quo is maintained regarding birthrates and other relevant factors, Jews may lose their majority in this combined area within a decade, according to demographics experts such as Hebrew University's Sergio Della Pergolla.[7] A withdrawal could remove the demographic threat posed by Gaza's population, but only if the disengagement is recognized by the international community as complete. Any hint that the withdrawal is partial would leave a window open for Israel's critics to argue that it remains responsible for Palestinians in Gaza.

While Israel's interests in leaving Gaza are clear, the benefits it would accrue if Gaza were declared a Palestinian state—or a proto- or mini-state—are less plain. On the one hand, Israel could demand that an internationally recognized Palestinian state fulfill its obligations like any other state. Moreover, facilitating the creation of such a state could improve Israel's diplomatic standing in the international community. And for those Israelis who believe that the problems posed by the West Bank are intractable, statehood would transform the conflict into a state-to-state border dispute—a less controversial and inflammatory relationship than that of occupier to occupied.

On the other hand, Israel is skeptical about the claim that statehood would temper Palestinian motivations for violence, particularly when issues such as Jerusalem and refugees have not been resolved. In fact, many Israelis believe that Palestinian violence is driven more by the "provocative" fact of Israel's existence than by the absence of a Palestinian state. Moreover, once granted a state, Palestinians could demand rights that they believe are inherent to statehood, such as freedom to form a military and establish military alliances with other states.

Premature statehood in Gaza would thus impose increasing burdens and dangers on Israeli self-defense. For example, in order to preempt Palestinian claims of "invasion," every Israeli reprisal against a Palestinian attack would necessitate written notification to the UN that the response was in keeping with Article 51 of the UN Charter, which authorizes self-defense. Given its troubled relationship with the UN, Israel has good reason to be skeptical that the world body would legitimize such reprisals. Hence, Palestinian statehood in Gaza could deprive Israel of its present right under international law to conduct "preventive military operations in the Gaza Strip."[8] Ironically, given the disadvantages of premature mini-statehood in the eyes of Prime Minister Ariel Sharon, the historically anti-Oslo statesman may wind up asserting the validity of the Oslo Accords, which preserve Israeli control over Gaza airspace and waters and preclude unilateral declarations of statehood.[9]

Palestinian interests. The prospect of statehood in Gaza is a double-edged sword for the Palestinians as well. A state would be the embodiment of their long-held aspirations. Yet, they have won considerable international sympathy and prestige as a stateless people, and establishing a mini-state in the near future could have drawbacks. In their eyes, accepting statehood in Gaza and the northern West Bank could isolate those areas from the remainder of the West Back and dilute the case for statehood in the rest of the disputed territories. Statehood could also alleviate pressure on Israel to take responsibility for Palestinian humanitarian needs and weaken Palestinian demands for access to employment in Israel proper. Taken together, these concerns may well make Palestinians wary of declaring statehood in the short term.

Despite their caution, Palestinians will likely call on the UN to define the Israeli withdrawal in the fullest terms possible. Such a definition could include language such as the following: "The absence of Israeli military control of, alternatively, Gaza's international border with Egypt, seashore and airspace and the emergence of a viable sovereign authority to take over the responsibilities toward the Palestinian population residing in the Strip."[10] Creative thinking would be needed to reconcile this sort of definition with legitimate Israeli security requirements.

International interests. The global community desires stability in Gaza so that it can facilitate economic development—which in turn would further increase stability. Border security and access are important as well; international economic assistance can be provided only if foreign nationals have safe passage in and out of the territory. Finally, the international community wants clear definition of the rules governing Gaza, which would encourage outside parties toward effective assistance and investment.

Legal Status of Gaza after Withdrawal

What legal structure best lends itself to satisfying the above network of needs? One could engage in interminable debates about labels—about whether the legal status of postwithdrawal Gaza should be statehood proper, residual Israeli occupation, or some intermediate status. Yet, such debates tend to consume time and sow antagonism, when what is really required is a creative and practical meeting of minds.

All of the core interests discussed above can be addressed through the framework of the Roadmap. It is, after all, the one document accepted by all the parties. Moreover, it assumes the creation (in Phase II) of "an independent Palestinian state with provisional borders and attributes of sovereignty, based on the new constitution, as a way station to a permanent status settlement." The words "provisional borders and attributes of sovereignty" should help allay Palestinian fears that the Gaza withdrawal is the end of the road, while simultaneously reassuring Israel that eventual Palestinian statehood is not without limitations and will include nonmilitarization provisions. Moreover, because provisional statehood is delayed until Phase II, the Palestinians have ample incentive to carry through the crucial first phase, which requires fighting terrorism.

The legal status of Gaza during Phase I—after Israel withdraws but before provisional statehood—could be something similar to that accorded to areas under Palestinian Authority control during the Oslo years. Alternatively, Gaza could be given "intermediate" status like that applied to East

Timor. Then, by the time provisional statehood is reached in Phase II, such a designation would be of clear benefit to both sides: the Palestinians could begin to realize their national aspirations, and the Israelis would be assured of limitations on the sovereignty of their neighbor. Moreover, the stability and goodwill generated by such an arrangement would make the area conducive to international aid and involvement.

Alternatives to a Bilateral Accord

Both Sharon and Mahmoud Abbas have indicated a willingness to coordinate Israel's withdrawal from Gaza. Of course, there are different levels of coordination, ranging from technical operational cooperation on the pullout itself to mutual understandings about the postwithdrawal period in the political, security, and economic spheres, including the question of Gaza's legal status.[11] Hopefully, Israel and the Palestinian Authority will indeed coordinate the terms of the withdrawal and agree on the rules that will govern the territory following the pullout. Yet, what if they resist signing an agreement enshrining the terms of their coordination? Israel may not want to be partner to a "negotiation" per se, as a signed agreement would imply. For their part, the Palestinians may not want to sign any document that ratifies a "unilateral" Israeli plan, even if they are willing to abide by its terms.

Coordination is possible without a bilateral accord, but it will require mediation by a third party, preferably the United States. This mediator could employ any of four techniques to reach agreement. First, both parties could write a letter to the third party informing it of their respective compliance. Second, a third party could compose a "note for the record" codifying the terms to which the parties have informally agreed. Third, the Palestinians could issue a public statement making clear that they will be bound by the terms of the Israeli withdrawal, even absent a formal accord. Fourth, the two parties could propose a joint resolution to the UN Security Council, which would provide an international imprimatur for such an agreement. (As noted previously, a Security Council endorsement would have the value of providing clarity to what could be a confusing situation.)

The Political Horizon

The Palestinians have traditionally wanted the international community to be as explicit as possible when sketching out the contours of a final-status agreement. They believe that most countries view the territorial endgame as they do—namely, a return to the pre-1967 borders. When third parties articulate this vision, the Palestinians see it as favorable to their interests, believing that such precedents can be used to pressure Israel when final-status negotiations eventually occur.

As his administration came to a close, President Bill Clinton laid out the parameters of his personal vision of a final settlement—a vision that was similar to the pre-1967 map, requiring Israel to hand over the equivalent of 97 percent of territories occupied during the Six Day War. Of course, Yasser Arafat refused this territorial vision, rejecting Clinton's belief that Palestinian refugees should resettle in the new Palestinian state and give up their demands on Israel proper.

At the time, Clinton publicly stated that this vision was a personal view and should not be interpreted as permanent U.S. policy. Some believe that the Bush administration should adopt the so-called Clinton Parameters as official policy. Although the administration has pointedly refused to define its position on territory, it has made clear its position on other final-status issues. For example, George W. Bush was the first president to articulate U.S. support for a two-state solution. In his landmark June 24, 2002, speech, he laid out the following principles:

> Ultimately, Israelis and Palestinians must address the core issues that divide them if there is to be a real peace, resolving all claims and ending the conflict between them. This means that the Israeli occupation that began in 1967 will be ended through a settlement negotiated between the parties, based on UN Resolutions 242 and 338, with Israeli withdrawal to secure and recognized borders.[12]

Some critics of the president believe the phrase "the Israeli occupation that began in 1967 will be ended" is insufficient. They would prefer an explicit embrace of the Clinton Parameters with regard to territory, arguing that Bush already implicitly adopted Clinton's position on refugees in his April 14, 2004, policy letter to Sharon. In that letter, Bush indicated his belief that Palestinian refugees should be resettled in the future state of Palestine and that settlement blocs adjacent to the pre-1967 Green Line may eventually be annexed by Israel. (See appendix 8 for the full text of the Bush-Sharon correspondence. Also see appendix 9 for excerpts from the joint press conference that coincided with the correspondence.) An equivalent promise to the Palestinians with regard to the pre-1967 territories is only fair, these critics argue.

Yet, is such a move advisable in the current environment? Would it give the Palestinians incentive to fight terrorism? The answer is an unequivocal "no"—if issued in the period before a Gaza withdrawal, such a blueprint would only undermine key short-term dynamics and, even worse, gratuitously and prematurely energize hardliners on both sides. Indeed, a U.S.-proposed final-status map would cause a diplomatic earthquake. On the Israeli side, Sharon's withdrawal plan could fall apart. Both he and his Likud Party were outspoken opponents of Camp David 2000 and the Clinton Parameters, and he would likely be forced to come out against President Bush as well. Currently, Sharon is in a vulnerable position. He has been able to withstand determined internal opposition to his Gaza plan thus far, but only by depending on broad public support and a national unity government. A revival of the Clinton Parameters would be a windfall for his opponents in Likud. The government would almost certainly collapse, thereby thwarting Gaza disengagement.

Abbas's rule is no less vulnerable than Sharon's, and no less likely to suffer if the United States were to prematurely issue a final-status vision. Abbas may have democratic legitimacy, but he does not yet possess Arafat's authority. Such a U.S. move would strengthen his hardline opponents, given that it would imply his willingness to compromise on territory and refugees. When Bush wrote his letter to Sharon in April 2004, it was clearly done without Arafat's acquiescence; accordingly, the chairman did not suffer politically. Abbas, however, is perceived as having a much closer relationship with Washington and would therefore be seen as complicit in any U.S. final-status blueprint. Like Sharon, he would have to either shun the United States or make himself vulnerable to the hardliners in his midst. Neither option is attractive.

After the Gaza disengagement, the question of whether a U.S. blueprint would help or hurt the chances for progress should be taken up again. At that point, there can be a proper accounting of whether the withdrawal was successful, as defined by three key criteria: reduced violence, increased authority for Abbas, and continued stability within the Israeli coalition (the organizing principle of the current national unity government is disengagement). Even if disengagement yields otherwise favorable conditions, the United States will need to determine whom a blueprint would embolden more: moderates or their hardline critics.

In all cases, the idea of a blueprint must be assessed against its prospects for success. A blueprint issued in the wake of Gaza disengagement could succeed only if Arab states did what they would not do at the end of the Clinton presidency: publicly and unequivocally endorse compromises, especially on the key issues of refugees and shared sovereignty over Jerusalem holy sites. Such endorsement would provide critical domestic political cover for Abbas. Indeed, Arab willingness to publicly support difficult compromises should be a major part of any U.S. decision to issue territorial blueprints after a successful disengagement. If Arab states press Washington to engage in the peace process while choosing to remain on the sidelines, they will have no one to blame but themselves if their wishes are similarly sidelined. The United States cannot risk another failure similar to that of 2000. Washington gained little credit or advantage in the Arab world for pressing onward with the Clinton Parameters at a time when violence raged.

Notes

1. On January 2, 1954, Egypt codified Gaza's status and named an Egyptian military governor. Its cabinet consisted of six military officers and two civilians who reported to the Egyptian defense ministry. Yet, a newspaper article published only a year later stated, "Egypt has no legal claim to Gaza, and neither has Israel." George Weller, "Sad Little Booby Prize: Egypt and Israel Face War over Gaza Strip," *Washington Post*, June 28, 1955.

2. Benny Morris, *Israel's Border Wars, 1949–1956* (London: Oxford University Press, 1993), pp. 389–392.

3. "Here's Egypt's Stand on Two Chief Issues," *Chicago Tribune*, March 3, 1957.

4. "Egypt Moves to Take Over Rule of Gaza," *Chicago Tribune*, March 12, 1957; and Homer Bigart, "Egypt's Governor Enters Gaza Strip," *New York Times*, March 15, 1957. See also Chaim Herzog, *The Arab-Israeli Wars: War and Peace in the Middle East from the War of Independence through Lebanon*, rev. ed. (New York: Vintage, 1984), p. 140.

5. UN Department of Peacekeeping Operations, "UNEF Deployment," in *Middle East: UNEF 1—Background*. Available online (www.un.org/Depts/dpko/dpko/co_mission/unef1backgr2.html#four).

6. Israel's view of occupation is complex. Prime Minister Ariel Sharon has acknowledged that Israel occupies the people of Gaza, but Israel resists the notion that the land is occupied, arguing that there is no internationally recognized legal sovereign over the territory. Therefore, Israel has abided by the 1949 Fourth Geneva Convention's humanitarian provisions without accepting that it is bound to the convention de jure.

7. Joshua Brilliant, "Are 1.4 Million Palestinians Missing?" United Press International, January 30, 2005. See also Sergio Della Pergolla, *Demography in Israel/Palestine: Trends, Prospects, Policy Implications* (Jerusalem: Avraham Harman Institute of Contemporary Jewry, Hebrew University, 2001).

8. Claude Bruderlein, "Legal Aspects of Israel's Disengagement Plan under International Humanitarian Law," Program on Humanitarian Policy and Conflict Research, Harvard University, 2005, p. 14.

9. In the disengagement plan approved by the Israeli cabinet on June 6, 2004, article 7 of part 1 reads, "The process set forth in the plan is without prejudice to the relevant agreements between the State of Israel and the Palestinians. Relevant arrangements shall continue to apply." (See appendix 6 for the full text of the cabinet resolution. Also see appendix 7 for the text of Sharon's October 25, 2004, address to the Knesset, delivered before the legislature's vote on the disengagement plan.) This suggests that Israel has not withdrawn from the Oslo Accords. Before becoming prime minister, Sharon repeatedly criticized Oslo, though he has been careful never to rule the agreement invalid. Many in both Israel and the Bush administration have come to accept his criticism, preferring a performance-based rather than a timetable approach.

10. Bruderlein, "Legal Aspects of Israel's Disengagement Plan," p. 11.

11. If the objective is some form of statehood, Israel may seek to ensure that it reaches even broader understandings with the Palestinians regarding the postwithdrawal period (e.g., limits on alliances with countries like Iran; restrictions on weaponry).

12. "President Bush Calls for New Palestinian Leadership," transcript of a speech delivered at the White House, June 24, 2002. Available online (www.whitehouse.gov/news/releases/2002/06/20020624-3.html).

ASSESSING THE
SECURITY CHALLENGES

ISRAEL'S WITHDRAWAL WILL GIVE RISE TO A VARIETY OF NEW
security challenges both in and around Gaza. These problems must be pre-
dicted and addressed well in advance of the pullout. In theory, the end of
Israeli occupation should diminish Palestinian motivations for violence in
Gaza. Yet, violence could erupt nonetheless due to developments such as
social anarchy, increased importation of weapons from Egypt, or a reener-
gized rejectionist effort led by Hamas.

As mentioned in chapter 1, Hamas will be invigorated, not placated, by
Israeli disengagement. The group views the Jewish state's very existence as
a legitimate reason for armed action. Naturally, Hamas will aim to demonstrate its political relevance by boasting that its violent activities effectively
caused the withdrawal. In the short term, the group may seek to maintain
quiet in Gaza as an indication that withdrawal equals security. Yet, this
situation would not last long without a large-scale Israeli pullout from the
West Bank.

For its part, Israel, like any sovereign country, would never forswear the
right to retaliate if attacked following withdrawal. Even if it did, such a
submission would likely have the unintended consequence of encouraging
more attacks; Gaza radicals would correctly assume they could strike Israel
with impunity. Obviously, asking Israel to give up the right to defend itself
is both unfair and unwise. If the Palestinian Authority (PA) acts depend-
ably against terrorists in Gaza, however, Israel could (and should) avoid
intervening in what would then be regarded as internal Palestinian affairs.

Of course, Israel is not the only party whose interests are threatened by
Hamas and other rejectionist factions. Such groups pose a clear danger to
the PA. Accordingly, the PA must work with Israel to deter those elements
from crippling the prospects for security and economic revival in Gaza.
Continued violence in and around Gaza would also prevent the United
States and the international community from building on the momentum of
disengagement in order to advance their long-held aspirations toward peace.
Egypt, too, has a stake in ensuring that radicalism does not spill over its eastern frontier. Indeed, the danger of a chaotic Gaza should deeply trouble all of
the vested players. Fortunately, such chaos is preventable if the international

community takes early and determined security measures. This chapter will explore these measures in detail, illustrating how various parties can help ensure that Gaza emerges from disengagement with a degree of stability.

Gaza during the Intifada

Gaza's recent history underscores its potential for volatility. According to the Israeli Shin Bet, this tiny strip of land produced the following imposing statistics during the first four years of the intifada: 460 Qassam rockets fired at towns and villages inside Israel, 300 attempted infiltrations into Israel by suspected suicide bombers, and at least 98 smuggling tunnels dug from Egypt.[1] Israeli military analyst Ze'ev Schiff asserted that, in the eighteen months before July 2004, "around 4,900 Kalashnikov assault rifles, 330 antitank devices, 33 shells of various caliber, and five machine guns" were smuggled into Gaza through these tunnels.[2] In addition, "two tons of explosives and around 380,000 bullets have been illicitly brought into the Strip." Gaza was also the intended recipient of a star-crossed effort to smuggle weapons by sea. In January 2002, Israeli commandos intercepted a ship on the high seas bearing arms from Iran to the Palestinians. Aboard the *Karine-A* were nearly fifty tons of antitank mines and missiles, two tons of TNT and C-4 explosives, hundreds of rocket-propelled grenades and launchers, and numerous katyusha rockets.[3]

Gaza has been a favored gathering spot not just for weapons, but also for the terrorist leaders who ordain their use. It was in Gaza that Hamas spiritual leader Sheikh Ahmed Yassin recast suicide bombing as a sacred act. Indeed, Hamas has its strongest base of support there. Even apart from Hamas, hostility toward Israel runs deep among adherents of all Palestinian factions in Gaza. Although Israeli military operations in the Strip have been aimed at terrorists, they have also caused the deaths of many innocent Palestinian civilians. In addition, civilian infrastructure has been seriously damaged, and economic activity routinely disrupted. It is safe to say that ordinary Gazans will remain skeptical, at best, toward Israel long after the withdrawal.

Palestinian Action Items

The new Palestinian leadership clearly understands that its obligation to control violence in Gaza is a duty of self-interest, not one imposed by the

Roadmap merely for Israel's sake. Even during the height of the intifada, Mahmoud Abbas had the courage to publicly criticize what he called the "militarization of the intifada" as disastrous for Palestinians.[4] During his brief tenure as prime minister in 2003, he worked to secure a ceasefire that remained in force for fifty-two days. In a December 14, 2004, interview with the Arabic daily *al-Sharq al-Awsat,* he stated, "There is a need to take steps to distance the intifada from the weapons because the intifada is a legitimate right of the people in order to express its negation of the occupation, using popular and social means. This is what happened in the first intifada in the 1980s.... The use of weapons was harmful and it has to stop."[5] (See appendix 10 for a full translation of this interview. See also appendix 11 for a transcript of a related interview that Abbas gave to al-Jazeera in January 2005). Similarly, Prime Minister Ahmed Qurei repeatedly called for Palestinian security services to end the *fouda,* or chaos, that had gripped the Palestinian street, echoing Abbas's use of the term *foudat al-silah,* or "chaos of weapons."[6]

Both leaders know that continued terrorism, and the inevitable Israeli response, will only hurt any meaningful chance for Palestinian political and economic reform. Moreover, if security does not take root in Gaza, the chance for a peace process that eventually leads to large-scale Israeli withdrawal from the West Bank is unlikely. Accordingly, the PA should focus on four key action items: reforming its security services, brokering a general ceasefire, reviving security coordination with Israel, and halting incitement.

Implementing security reforms. The PA will not be able to control Gaza without reforming its security services. In December 2004, Abbas stated, "In all frankness, the Palestinian security apparatuses need reorganization and reform. There is a security vacuum. Therefore, we strive for unifying those bodies."[7] Successful reform will require three steps. First, the PA must consolidate its disparate services—more than a dozen in number—under a unified chain of command. Second, security personnel should undergo rigorous training with the goal of transforming highly politicized militias into a professional, uniform, skilled security force.[8] Third, the leadership itself must be reformed, with the goal of replacing political leaders with professional security officers.[9]

Establishing appropriate membership criteria for the security forces is crucial as well. Abbas would like to integrate members of Hamas and the Fatah al-Aqsa Martyrs Brigades into the reformed services as a way of co-opting rivals with the lure of salaries and authority. This temptation should be resisted. In some special cases, it might be advisable to pacify a given rival with a sinecure, but it would be a terrible mistake to integrate large numbers of such individuals into the security services, especially when rival forces still exist.[10] The danger of infiltration by adversaries would be too great. Numerous PA security personnel have already engaged in terrorist activities during their "off hours," making themselves legitimate targets for Israeli attacks. If Israel had reason to believe that reformed security services were infiltrated, bilateral coordination would become considerably more difficult.

Some preliminary reforms have already taken place. In spring 2004, under heavy international pressure from the Quartet and other parties, the PA agreed to pay its security personnel in an orderly fashion. Security officers opened bank accounts, and their salaries were deposited monthly. On the surface, this may not seem like a noteworthy measure. Previously, however, Yasser Arafat had employed an entirely arbitrary system under which PA security chiefs had full discretion as to whether, when, and how much to pay their subordinates.

The international community has also shown signs of assuming its key role in facilitating security reform. Egypt has committed to training some Palestinian security officials. Moreover, in early 2004, Britain created a "central operations room" in Ramallah through which different security forces could communicate with one another, issue and receive intelligence reports, and dispatch directives. Although the success of this measure was limited, the precedent of professionalization remains significant.[11] In November 2004, the PA hinted that a similar operations center would be established in Gaza.[12]

Brokering a general ceasefire. The post-Arafat era ushered in hopes for a general ceasefire between Palestinian terrorist factions and Israel, culminating in an agreement reached in Cairo on March 18, 2005. Leading up to the agreement, Abbas held a series of meetings with Hamas, Palestinian Islamic Jihad (PIJ), and various leaders from the al-Aqsa Martyrs Brigades. Afterward, he declared that the verbal understandings he had reached with these groups constituted a commitment to a ceasefire; he did not obtain such agreements from smaller militant factions, however.

In characterizing the agreement, the rejectionist groups used the term *tahdiya*, or cooling off, which they differentiate from a truce, or *hudna*. In their eyes, a *hudna* is a mutual agreement with Israel, with all the associated obligations thereof, while a *tahdiya* can be a unilateral Palestinian decision. Originally, the parties agreed to a thirty-day *tahdiya*; the agreement was eventually extended, despite a PIJ suicide bombing in Tel Aviv in late February (in response to an alleged Israeli "provocation").

As mentioned previously, Abbas managed to uphold a fifty-two-day truce during his abortive premiership in summer 2003. Yet, any future *hudna* is likely to fail unless precise terms are delineated on paper. This would not be an easy task, given that Israel and Hamas will not sit at the same negotiation table or sign a common document. Parallel documents—one between the PA and rejectionist factions, and another between the PA and Israel—are not as important as ensuring that Israeli-Palestinian understandings are precise. That is, with Egypt's help, the PA must come to specific understandings with the various militant factions, with the further understanding that Israel will respect these terms. Abbas has already begun to hold talks with Hamas and other rejectionist groups, and Egypt has organized meetings in Cairo.

To avoid the mistakes that led to the collapse of the 2003 *hudna*, two sets of potential misunderstandings must be avoided. First, all parties must adopt a clear, shared stance on the status of Palestinian areas still under Israeli control. During the 2003 ceasefire, Israel understood that Hamas was proscribed from carrying out violent activities in such areas according to the terms of the *hudna*, while Hamas believed the disputed territories were still valid targets. The PA blamed Israel for Hamas's misunderstanding, since the area was, in effect, under Israel's control.[13]

Second, clear ground rules must be established with regard to "ticking bomb" scenarios. That is, the PA should commit to responding immediately when Israel has information about an imminent terrorist operation, sparing Israel from taking any potentially provocative action.[14] This condition is reasonable—if Israel is prohibited from arresting such "ticking bombs," then it has the right to insist that the Palestinians foil impending attacks themselves. For their part, the Palestinians have the right to receive intelligence about imminent attacks far enough in advance to allow them to respond. Such a policy could help bring an end to Israel's practice of targeted assassinations. It would also allow Israel to retain its legitimate right to self-defense without being self-defeating: i.e., if the PA acts, Israel will not have to. A similar cooperative approach was successfully employed—with some notable exceptions—during the Oslo years of the 1990s. It collapsed, however, with the outbreak of the intifada.

Moreover, in the early stages of a ceasefire, the Palestinians should work with Israel on security understandings that preserve Gaza's infrastructure. Such agreements could be similar in tone to those made at the beginning of the intifada proscribing the targeting of water supplies. Israel should convey any such commitments to those donors willing to sponsor "protected" projects. Israel's interests on this point are self-evident: destruction of infrastructure would only increase Palestinian unemployment, which would in turn provoke international pressure on Israel to accept greater numbers of Palestinian workers—an undertaking that it regards as a security risk.

Ceasefire understandings should also focus on rocket attacks, which will likely remain the most significant Gaza-based threat to Israel (whether in the form of homemade Qassams or smuggled katyushas).[15] Without adequate security arrangements, rockets fired from northern Gaza could conceivably hit the Ashkelon oil refinery and other strategic Israeli assets. In order to ensure an effective, durable ceasefire, the PA should take action against Qassam rocket workshops and launching pads and prevent the smuggling of foreign missiles. Creating a public climate that delegitimizes such attacks is crucial as well. Unlike Arafat, Abbas has campaigned on the platform that violence is counterproductive, and he can genuinely claim a mandate on this issue.

Israelis and Palestinians are bound to have contrasting philosophies about whether a ceasefire is an end in itself or a bridge to the broader objective of disarming radicals. Israel clearly favors the latter view, while the Palestinians often tend toward the former. In the early stages of a truce, however, both sides will agree that a military showdown between the PA and Hamas is unlikely. Unlike during the 2003 *hudna*, Sharon did not demand that Abbas engage in such a showdown immediately following Arafat's death in November 2004. This was a marked departure for Sharon, perhaps reflecting his understanding of the fragility of internal Palestinian dynamics and Abbas's legitimacy. To be sure, a PA-Hamas confrontation does not have to be massive in order to be effective—closing rocket labs, arresting key operatives, removing imams who incite violence, and reconditioning Palestinian views on violence would be important first steps. Still, at some point after the Gaza withdrawal, a showdown between the PA and rejectionist factions seems inevitable. It is terrorism, after all, that has prevented the formation of a Palestinian state until now, and Palestinian national aspirations may be permanently thwarted if terrorist groups are permitted to operate with impunity in Palestinian society.

Reviving security coordination. U.S. Army general William "Kip" Ward, Washington's point man in the effort to restructure the PA security services, has also been tasked with reviving the dialogue that existed between Israeli and Palestinian security personnel during the 1990s. At the core of such cooperation are intelligence exchanges. Yet, Ward's background signals an important change on this front. When the CIA was in charge of security coordination during the 1990s, it viewed Palestinian attacks primarily through the prism of intelligence. Consequently, Israelis believed that their own counterterrorism concerns sometimes received short shrift.[16] They are certainly happier now that a U.S. army officer is in charge. For its part, the CIA viewed its responsibilities in this area as particularly difficult, so it may find the new arrangement more satisfactory as well.

The format of security coordination deserves special consideration. During the 1990s, such coordination was often trilateral, with the United States as the third party. A similar three-pronged structure could be usefully revived in the current environment. Alternatively, a combination of bilateral and trilateral formats could optimize prospects for cooperation, with near-daily bilateral contacts and monitored, perhaps weekly, follow-up talks with the United States. Such an approach could minimize the prospect of mutual recrimination.

Whatever the structure of coordination, it is critical that both Israel and the Palestinians be held accountable for their security commitments. As Dennis Ross, the lead U.S. peace envoy during the 1990s, has acknowledged, failure on this front contributed to the collapse of the peace process in 2000–2001.[17] In order to ensure accountability, the United States must agree to publicize any failures by either side, since both parties fear open U.S. accusations of nonperformance. The threat of negative publicity could be an effective deterrent to diplomatic intransigence, but it would require a strong commitment of American political will to be a meaningful instrument of policy.

Halting incitement. The absence of violence is not enough—the nascent peace process requires an environment free of hate-filled calls to violence. In the immediate term, this means modifying government-run media in Palestinian areas, reviewing the PA educational curriculum, and scrutinizing Friday sermons in mosques. As mentioned in chapter 1, Abbas took a positive first step by calling out Radwan Abu Ayash, head of the Palestinian Broadcasting Company, in the immediate aftermath of Arafat's death.

He urged Ayash to avoid airing music videos glorifying those who embark on "martyrdom" operations against Israel, as well as news coverage referring to suicide bombers as "martyrs."[18] Shortly thereafter, the government-run television channel broadcast an unusual sermon at an important Gaza mosque that focused on Islam as a religion of tolerance.[19] The sermon was attended by Abbas and other senior PA figures.

Privately, PA officials acknowledge that Hamas poses as much of a threat to the PA as it does to Israel, and that a great deal of the antagonism that the group represents has been stirred in mosques by imams who receive PA salaries. These officials argue that the PA must be alert to such incitement. Indeed, as early as 1996 they raised the prospect of removing certain hardcore preachers from the territories. Clearly, creating a climate of coexistence will take a long time, but the PA can help facilitate this process by demonstrating in words as well as actions that the path of nonviolence is more desirable.

The International Dimension

Israelis and Palestinians cannot handle the security challenges of the Gaza handover on their own. Even if a ceasefire holds, deep skepticism will remain in Israel and abroad about the PA's ability and willingness to sustain policing efforts in Gaza. Israel is thus faced with an analytical conundrum: Israelis favor unilateral disengagement from Gaza in large part because they do not trust the Palestinians, but this same mistrust leads Israelis to wonder whether the PA can prevent the postwithdrawal militarization of Gaza. Because of these suspicions, Israel would prefer to closely monitor Gaza's borders after disengagement, but such monitoring could lead some parties to declare the withdrawal incomplete. Indeed, any lingering Israeli authority over Gaza could endanger the prospects of a UN Security Council certification of the withdrawal. Hence, Israelis face the formidable challenge of avoiding a zero-sum situation—they must devise a scenario whereby their security is guaranteed without them having to physically control all activity along the Gaza perimeter.

The international community can help resolve these conundrums, but its precise role requires careful consideration. Some have suggested dispatching a NATO force similar to that deployed in the Balkans. Unrestricted international intervention would be deeply problematic, however.

To better understand the possible pitfalls of international involvement, it is useful to review the historical role of international forces in the Arab-Israeli conflict. Such forces have been most successful in contexts where the warring parties had already made a political commitment to secure peace. In contrast, international forces have been useless in situations where either side lacked the political will to enforce such a peace. Success stories include the U.S.-led Multinational Force and Observers (MFO) in the Sinai, formed in the wake of the 1979 Egyptian-Israeli peace treaty, and the UN Disengagement Observer Force (UNDOF) in the Golan Heights, deployed after the 1974 disengagement agreement between Israel and Syria.[20] On each of these fronts, the multinational force was successful because the separated parties were committed to peace.

In contrast, one ongoing failure is the international force on the Lebanon-Israel border, created by the UN in the wake of Israel's 1978 Litani Operation. Israel views the UN Interim Force in Lebanon (UNIFIL) as an entirely futile entity because it has failed to prevent Hizballah attacks. UN officials argue that UNIFIL has no mandate as a fighting force, but is instead charged with monitoring the situation. This disparity illustrates the fundamental problem with interposing a multinational force between hostile parties.

The rationale for internationalization should be based on the proper premise. If the political will exists to curb radicalism, the technical capabilities of a multinational force can in fact be useful. If the parties lack such will, however, technical assistance is beside the point, and soldiers from third countries may find themselves caught in the crossfire without a calming strategy. Few countries would want to commit their forces under such conditions.[21] The main challenge in maintaining ceasefires is one of commitment, not capability. The Palestinians must demonstrate adequate political will before they can expect to address their technical limitations through the international provision of additional funds, resources, training, diplomatic support, and so forth.

To date, no country has volunteered to dispatch troops to volatile Gaza. Even otherwise interested third parties have not exactly fought for the privilege of sending their forces there. For example, although Egypt has a clear interest in a stable Gaza, Foreign Minister Ahmed Aboul Gheit stated in late 2004, "We are not offering Egyptian troops or personnel into the Palestinian areas."[22]

Moreover, Israel is wary of permitting foreign troops in the Strip, believing that they may unwittingly serve as a shield for militant groups.

If an outside force were deployed, it would make Israeli retaliatory self-defense measures almost impossible. Israel would be caught between two unacceptable choices: absorb Palestinian attacks or risk hitting a third party (and likely a close ally) in a crossfire. Israel fears that even a well-intentioned U.S.-led intervention could endanger its cherished alliance with Washington and provide rejectionist groups with further incentive to launch attacks. Additionally, support for internationalization remains low among Israelis, as the unhappy legacy of international intervention in Lebanon has been seared into their national memory.[23]

Among Palestinian officials, international intervention holds some superficial attraction because it seems to promise a quick end to Israeli military occupation. Yet, even Palestinian support for a foreign military presence is highly conditional. Most Palestinians want international forces dispatched along the pre-1967 lines, arguing that anything less could legitimize Israeli occupation and prevent them from mounting any resistance. If foreign soldiers were stationed deeper inside Palestinian territory, militants could depict them as Israeli surrogates, protectors of the status quo, rather than as peacekeepers. Few Palestinians would trust the peacekeepers' promises to withdraw within a defined period, and the longer they remained, the more hostility they would generate on the streets of Gaza. In other words, such forces could find themselves caught between Palestinian resentment and Israeli mistrust.

Despite these obstacles, there is a proper international role in securing Gaza. Specifically, the international community could take on at least three military-security roles that would be largely free of the above problems. First, foreign troops could help train the PA security services to better discharge their duties. Second, such troops could provide assistance at the Gaza-Egypt border. Third, international actors could create a consulting service that would bolster Israeli and Palestinian confidence and perhaps pave the way for a multinational force to help secure the future Gaza seaport and airport. Key facets of the latter two roles are examined in the sections that follow.

Halting Tunnel Smuggling

The international community can play a key role in allaying Israeli fears that the Palestinians will continue to smuggle weapons into Gaza from Egypt through tunnels at the Rafah border. Within the first month after coming to power, Abbas's government made successful preliminary efforts to curb such smuggling.[24] Nevertheless, as discussed previously, Israel has ample precedent for its suspicions.

If effective border arrangements are not worked out, senior Israeli defense officials have made their intentions clear. According to Defense Minister Shaul Mofaz, "The [Israel Defense Forces'] deployment around the Gaza perimeter will prevent terrorists from entering Israel. Control of the air and sea will remain in our hands.... We will also control the Philadelphia route between Rafah and the Egyptian border."[25] (The Philadelphia Corridor is a sandy strip, six miles long and a hundred yards wide, sandwiched between Gaza and Egypt.) Mofaz's position was echoed in the Israeli cabinet's revised disengagement plan of June 6, 2004. (See appendix 6 for the full text of the plan. See also appendix 12 for a summary of a February 2005 cabinet meeting in which further revisions were approved.)[26] Sharon has repeatedly stated that he seeks an eventual withdrawal from the corridor, but the Israeli defense establishment has insisted that Israel remain there until an acceptable solution to Palestinian weapons smuggling has been found. Israel shelved the idea of creating an eighty-foot-deep, three-mile-long seawater trench along the corridor, which would have required demolishing anywhere from 200 to 3,000 Palestinian homes. Instead, it is erecting a less invasive barrier of concrete and fences.[27] Whether such measures alone will serve as a deterrent remains to be seen.

If possible, steps should be taken so that Israel does not have to remain in the Philadelphia Corridor indefinitely. The harmful consequences of a continued Israeli presence there after Gaza withdrawal would be twofold. First, Hamas and others would likely object to the continuing "occupation" and turn the corridor into a flashpoint for conflict, launching attacks against Israeli soldiers stationed there.[28] Israel would of course retaliate, and the net effect would be instability. Second, critics would likely discredit the disengagement, and the possibility of obtaining international endorsement for the withdrawal could fade.

Operating on the Egyptian Side of the Border

Although the prospect of outside forces remaining in any part of Gaza is highly problematic, Israel's legitimate security concerns must nevertheless be addressed. One solution is to focus on the Egyptian side of the Gaza border—a far more stable environment for an international force. In chaotic and unpredictable Gaza, such a force could easily find itself targeted by radicals. The Egyptian side of Rafah in particular is more operationally hospitable than the more densely populated Palestinian side. Operating on the Egyptian side also has the advantage of employing the expertise of the Egyptian security services. Moreover, the demilitarization and force-limitation provisions of its 1979 peace treaty with Israel obligate Egypt to provide security on its side of the border—an obligation that should continue at Rafah following the Israeli withdrawal from Gaza.[29]

Egypt is uniquely positioned to deal with tunnel smuggling at Rafah. Clans living on both sides of the border transformed the smuggling of trade goods into a cottage industry in the aftermath of the peace treaty. Today, the tunnels are routinely used to smuggle weapons as well as goods.[30] Only the Egyptians, with their knowledge of the local geography and culture, can effectively uncover and police the tunnels.

In light of these factors, the international community should adopt a two-pronged approach to Egyptian involvement: upgrading Egyptian security personnel at Rafah and extending the scope of the Sinai MFO. Israel and Egypt essentially agreed to the first measure in December 2004, when Cairo pledged to upgrade its lightly armed police in the Rafah area to 750 border security personnel, with deployment to begin in spring 2005.[31] The two sides are planning to exchange letters to this effect, thereby sidestepping any need to amend their 1979 peace treaty.[32] Israeli defense officials believe that Egypt, which has superior knowledge of the area and therefore better ability to thwart potential attacks, could enhance security by deploying intelligence personnel to the Egyptian part of Rafah and areas to the immediate south.

An important ancillary benefit of the joint effort to upgrade Egyptian border security has been closer coordination between the Egyptian and Israeli security establishments—an intimacy noticeably absent during most of the quarter-century since the signing of the peace treaty. This coordination helped facilitate a broader thaw between the two countries in late 2004. Manifestations of this thaw included Egypt's willingness to return its ambassador to Israel after a four-and-a-half year absence during the intifada; its release of suspected spy Azzam Azzam; its willingness to sign a Qualifying Industrial Zone pact with Israel; and its hosting of the February 2005 Sharm al-Sheikh summit attended by Sharon and Abbas.

Making Use of the MFO

Operating under U.S. civilian and military leadership and headquartered in Rome, the Sinai MFO is composed of approximately 2,000 troops from eleven countries (including two U.S. battalions with about 700 personnel each). It came into being in 1981 when the UN refused to endorse the Egyptian-Israeli peace treaty. Its mission is to ensure that the terms of the treaty are enforced and to preclude the need for a massive remilitarization of Sinai. The MFO has been remarkably successful in ensuring calm along the border, a record of accomplishment that may give both the force itself and its participating countries the confidence needed to take on an expanded mission.

Extending the scope of the Sinai MFO through deployments to the Egyptian side of the Rafah area would have two important benefits: raising the diplomatic cost for Egypt if it failed to fulfill its security obligations, and easing the Egyptian security burden by observing and reporting on smuggling activity around Rafah. Most important, the MFO already operates on what is known as "the IB (International Border) Road." It also maintains a number of adjacent temporary observation posts that vary from around-the-clock capability to daytime use for fixed and mobile teams. Technically, its mandate already extends just beyond the Gaza border, as stipulated in the military annex of the Egyptian-Israeli peace treaty.

Given their familiarity with the MFO, Egypt and Israel would likely be receptive to its involvement in securing the Egypt-Gaza border. Senior Egyptian military officials, including intelligence chief Gen. Omar Suleiman, have already indicated that they would welcome MFO deployment in this area.[33] Senior U.S. officials have been supportive of the idea as well and are optimistic about its feasibility. Even senior Israeli security officials, who are most comfortable with an international force if it is under U.S. leadership, have privately voiced support for the idea, as have certain Palestinian officials.

An obvious advantage of the MFO is that it already exists. Establishing a new organization—with all its attendant bureaucracy—would require a major investment of time. The MFO itself took nearly a year-and-a-half to establish because it entailed persuading eleven countries to join and hammering out procedures agreeable to both Egypt and Israel. Moreover, with contributions of $17 million apiece from Egypt, Israel, and the United States, the MFO is well funded and maintained. Ironing out the legal issues involved in expanding the MFO's mandate could be handled through a simple exchange of letters between the three nations; there would be no need to re-ratify the Egyptian-Israeli peace treaty.

The MFO's mission at the Gaza border would be somewhat different from its current assignment, so merely diverting personnel to new locations may be insufficient; additional personnel would be required. Accordingly, the parties must decide whether the Gaza force should be an additive to the extant MFO or a separate MFO of its own, at least from a legal standpoint. Such distinctions could be resolved relatively quickly.[34]

Apart from the general desirability of using the Sinai MFO, there are several factors that make alternative forces undesirable. First, although the Israelis would accept a U.S.-led force akin to the existing MFO, they would not accept any UN-commanded force for a sensitive mission that required them to take on security risks. Despite occasional examples of cooperation, the relationship between the UN and Israel during the last few decades has been largely adversarial. Given the history of frequent weapons smuggling from Egypt into Gaza, there must be a high level of trust between a multinational force and all the parties—particularly Israel, since its security is most at stake.

NATO is not an attractive alternative either, given that it is beholden to the consensus of its twenty-six member states. Obtaining such consensus for a Gaza mission would be difficult; historically, issues related to the Arab-Israeli conflict have tended to strain transatlantic ties. Moreover, any substantial change in NATO missions requires the approval of all member states. It is therefore difficult to envision the rapid establishment of a new NATO force for Gaza, and even more difficult to imagine such a force being flexible enough to adapt quickly in the face of shifting conditions on the ground. Moreover, as with the UN, there is insufficient trust between Israel and many European NATO members to quell Israeli concerns that a NATO force would be politicized. A NATO role may well be called for in the future, but it does not appear viable in the short term.

Another advantage of using the existing MFO is that it would not meaningfully encumber an already overburdened U.S. military. While the United States would have to add some personnel (most likely from the Army Corps of Engineers, to provide technical assistance with policing smuggling tunnels), the bulk of new forces could come from other MFO member states. In this case, U.S. leadership is more essential than U.S. troops.

In addition, an upgraded MFO outfitted with seismic technology could be more effective at detecting and destroying tunnels than Egypt, the PA, or Israel. In an October 2004 report, Human Rights Watch criticized Israeli methods of closing smuggling tunnels and offered the following suggestions to the Israel Defense Forces (IDF):

> No one method is guaranteed to work in all situations, but different techniques can compensate for each other's shortcomings, and overall conditions in Rafah favor the IDF: Only four kilometers of the border run alongside Rafah, and tunnel depth is limited by the water table—approximately forty-five meters in the camp. In this environment, the IDF could install an array of underground seismic sensors along the border. Known as an 'underground fence,' this method has successfully detected digging activity on the U.S.-Mexico border. Other methods, such as electromagnetic induction and ground-penetrating radar, could be used to detect tunnels."[35]

The "underground fence" solution could be implemented by the MFO, with technical expertise from the U.S. Army Corps of Engineers.[36]

For all of the above reasons, the MFO is the most logical candidate to head a multinational mission. Although the PA is not party to the Egyptian-Israeli peace treaty, its endorsement of an MFO deployment on the Egyptian side of the Gaza border would nevertheless be crucial. Moreover, any UN Security Council resolution ratifying Israel's withdrawal from Gaza should also include a provision making clear that the world body endorses any new MFO arrangement.

Building Confidence through Consultation

In addition to training PA forces and securing the Egyptian side of the Gaza border, the international community should create a consultative mechanism to encourage security-related trust and coordination between Israelis and Palestinians. Israel, Egypt, the PA, and the MFO would require some formal method for discussion of ongoing security concerns. Such a mechanism is already prescribed for Egypt and Israel in Annex I of their peace treaty, and it can be extended to Gaza-related consultations with the multinational force, the United States, and the PA. The separate revival of U.S.-Israeli-Palestinian security coordination is vital as well; without regular communication, misunderstandings are likely. These myriad consultations would need to be carefully structured, of course. For example, Israel would not want its separate Sinai security discussions with Egypt to be filtered through the Palestinians.

The logical site for regular (perhaps daily) consultations is Kerem Shalom, the border area adjacent to the southeast corner of Gaza, where Israel plans to relocate its portion of the Gaza border crossing (thus avoiding violent flare-ups at Rafah). In particular, Egyptian, Israeli, Palestinian, and MFO officials should have a dedicated operations room to discuss any security-related problems and allay suspicions.

Airport and Seaport: Now or Later?

Ensuring the security of a Gaza airport and seaport is an even thornier proposition than monitoring the Egypt-Gaza border, since it would require a multinational force to be deployed inside Gaza proper. Such an arrangement would likely make participating countries nervous, even if their troops were assigned to defined locations on the periphery. Only after Gaza has been calm for some time would multinational forces willingly step in to help.

Ongoing consultations (again, at Kerem Shalom) could be a helpful confidence-building measure as Israel weighs the possibility for either an enhanced MFO or PA role in securing a Gaza seaport and airport.[37] Circumspection is required, however, because Israel will be hesitant to take on another Gaza challenge until it is convinced that its security is not in jeopardy. At the same time, one could argue that a decision on the security administration of Gaza ports should be made early, to give the Gaza economy a stabilizing shot in the arm. By this argument, if the force tasked with this mission came under attack or failed in its security objectives, the ports could always be closed and the force redeployed. Both approaches should be considered.

Given that most Palestinian exports are to Israel, not overseas, a Palestinian seaport is needed to increase international trade and promote Palestinian independence from the Israeli economy. Ideally, an international supervisor would monitor the security aspects of such a port. At the Wye River talks in 1998, then–foreign minister Ariel Sharon expressed his support for a Palestinian seaport. Before the intifada broke out, the parties hammered out an agreement for security terms at a Gaza port, but it was never implemented. Currently, no seaport exists, and it could take years to build one.

The World Bank has suggested the establishment of a "roll-on, roll-off" seaport in Gaza, which is easier to build than a full-service deep-sea port, albeit more limited in its capabilities. Such a facility could be supplemented by secure loading at Egypt's Port Said, which regularly handles transshipments to Europe. For nearby third-party transshipments, the Sinai town of al-Arish is only a few miles from Gaza. There, too, an MFO or other third party could inspect shipments and facilitate movement of cargo that has been reliably sealed at its point of origin.

Although an MFO could provide perimeter security for such a facility, actual cargo management would need to be contracted out to commercial professionals such as Lloyd's of London. Lloyd's worked with the Aqaba Port Authority in handling transshipment inspections following the 1991 passage of UN Security Council Resolution 665, which called for naval enforcement of sanctions against Saddam Hussein and remained in place for a decade. The deployment of professionals familiar with cargo inspection and management in conflict areas is preferable to using soldiers—both from a technical view and in terms of assuaging Israel's security concerns. Still, in the absence of comprehensive Israeli-Palestinian security agreements, Israel will remain wary of replacing its own authority with any third party.

Until trust is reestablished, it might be best to simply give the Palestinians a temporary pier in the Israeli port of Ashdod, only a few miles north of Gaza. Palestinian goods have been exported from Ashdod for many years. Currently, Palestinians complain that their exports do not receive equal treatment there. Hence, they would likely insist that Israel minimize, if not eliminate, its controls on any temporary pier at Ashdod, while Israel would insist on preserving security inspections and safeguards. As a compromise, the pier could be supervised by a combination of an MFO alongside a reputable international firm such as Lloyd's.

Whatever port solution is chosen, the Palestinians will remain dependent on Ashdod for quite some time. Hence, in the short term, and perhaps beyond, there is no reason why Ashdod cannot serve as their main port. New arrangements can be implemented to the mutual satisfaction of both parties. For example, Israel could create a rail line between Ashdod and Erez in order to facilitate movement of goods from the Gaza border to the port. A rail line already exists between Ashdod and Ashkelon, so only about a few more miles of track would be needed to reach Erez.

The Ashdod idea is a short-term fix, a step toward increasing Palestinian trade, and its implementation would answer those critics who claim that Israel wants to limit Palestinian exports for protectionist rather than security reasons. If confidence in Gaza's enduring stability increased, however, Israel would need to consider allowing the MFO, working with a reputable international security and cargo management company, to take over security at a separate Palestinian seaport. The same criterion could be applied to reactivating the Gaza airport. In the meantime, alternative airport arrangements outside Gaza would be necessary, with a focus on cities such as Amman, Cairo, Tel Aviv, and perhaps al-Arish in Sinai. Again, both approaches to the question of a Gaza seaport and airport—either activating them early, under the security management of an MFO, or fashioning temporary solutions outside Gaza until the area stabilizes—have validity.

Preventing Seaborne Smuggling

As the text of its disengagement plan makes clear, Israel is concerned that the PA lacks the political will to effectively patrol the Gaza coast and prevent the smuggling of weapons by sea. Consequently, Israel declared that it will continue to patrol the coast itself following withdrawal. Ideally, though, the Sinai MFO should take on that role (if not immediately, then down the road), provided it is willing to act in close consultation with the U.S. Sixth Fleet, the Egyptian and Israeli navies, and the PA. The MFO already has several sea vessels at its disposal, but this expanded duty would require participating countries, primarily the United States, to provide additional assistance.

Ensuring Safe Passage between Gaza and the West Bank

The Oslo provision that has proven most difficult to implement is the idea of "safe passage" between the West Bank and Gaza. Implementing it was problematic during the 1990s and impossible during the intifada. The idea has become anathema to Israeli military planners, given the threat of suicide bombers using it as a cover to reach vulnerable targets in Israel (e.g., crowded Tel Aviv bus terminals). In fact, Israel's security fence and disengagement plan were developed with the common goal of preventing incursions into Israeli urban areas. At the same time, the Palestinian humanitarian costs associated with the lack of safe passage are substantial.

Sharon has indicated that he would consider establishing train service between Gaza and the West Bank. In any case, Israel would need to handle security arrangements for passage between the territories itself, at least until it could trust a multinational force at the perimeter of Gaza to take on such a role. As Israelis and Palestinians made progress, more sophisticated ideas could be considered, such as an elevated highway or underground tunnel financed by third parties. These solutions would take many years to implement, however, and interim solutions must be found to the satisfaction of both parties. Such provisional solutions are discussed in chapter 4.

Notes

1. Shin Bet, "Four Years of Conflict: Israel's War against Terrorism," October 3, 2004, posted on the Israeli ministry of foreign affairs website (www.mfa.gov.il). See also Doron Almog (Israel's top military commander in Gaza for much of the intifada), "Tunnel-Vision in Gaza," *Middle East Quarterly* (Summer 2004), pp. 3–11; available online (www. meforum.org/article/630). For more on the security environment in Gaza, see Almog's *The West Bank Fence: A Vital Component in Israel's Strategy of Defense* (Washington, D.C.: The Washington Institute for Near East Policy, March 2004).

2. Ze'ev Schiff, "Palestinian Groups in Gaza Amassing Arms Ahead of Withdrawal," *Haaretz* (Tel Aviv), September 19, 2004.

3. James Bennet, "Skipper Ties Cargo to Arafat's Group," *New York Times*, January 8, 2002. This article cites the skipper of the *Karine-A*, identified as "Captain Akawi," stating that the plan was to "unload in Gaza." Three other documented seaborne infiltrations were attempted prior to the *Karine-A*, all of which failed (e.g., see "Boat Containing Weapons Found off Israel," CNN.com, May 7, 2001; available online at http://archives.cnn. com/2001/WORLD/meast/05/07/mideast.boat/index.html).

4. Abbas has been unique among Palestinian critics of the intifada. During his short-lived premiership in summer 2003, he argued that the intifada was not only politically counterproductive to the Palestinians, but also morally wrong. His public comments to this effect (on June 24, 2003, at the Aqaba summit with President George W. Bush and Israeli prime minister Ariel Sharon) led to a sharp decline in his popularity at home.

5. Nasser Qadih, "Stressing the Need to Stop the Militarization of the Intifada," *al-Sharq al-Awsat* (London), December 14, 2004.

6. Ibid.

7. Ibid.

8. Hatem Abdul Khader (Palestine Legislative Council member), interview by author, Ramallah, West Bank, August 16, 2004. Khader is active in the Fatah young guard and has held talks to discuss the prospects of Hamas accepting sharp limitations on its capabilities. He also stated that the key to reform is depoliticizing the PA security services.

9. The PA could give a clear signal of such institutional change by bringing to justice those Palestinians who murdered three U.S. government contractors in Gaza in 2003. Yasser Arafat's failure to do so led the U.S. Agency for International Development to suspend its infrastructure project in the Strip.

10. After its 1948 War of Independence, Israel's new security forces integrated some operatives from nonmainstream groups such as the Irgun and the Stern Gang (e.g. Yitzhak Shamir). Yet, such integration occurred only after these and other prestatehood militant groups had been dismantled.

11. In a December 15, 2004, interview with the author, senior British officials familiar with the central operations room stated that it had helped thwart half a dozen attacks during 2004.

12. After a Council of Ministers meeting on November 20, 2004, the PA announced the following: "The [prime minister] discussed with the ministers the decisions made by the [National Security Council] in their last meeting, especially those related to the strengthening of the security apparatus performance in the realm of maintaining order and the rule of law. The Council demanded that the NSC give priority to imposing order, promoting teamwork, and devising the laws under which the security agencies function. The Council was also informed of the recent decisions made by the NSC concerning the forming of a unified executive force that will begin its work in Gaza as a first step."

13. Brig. Gen. Michael Herzog, interview by author, November 30, 2004. General Herzog served as top military aide to Israeli defense minister Shaul Mofaz during summer 2003.

14. On August 14, 2003, in the midst of the *hudna,* Israeli forces killed a PIJ militant named Muhammad Sidr in Hebron. Israeli officials considered him a "ticking bomb," meaning he was on his way to conduct a suicide mission against Israelis. According to them, it was their intention to arrest him, but when he resisted, he was killed in the exchange of fire. Five days later, a suicide bomber attacked an Israeli bus in Jerusalem, killing at least twenty (including six children). Hamas and PIJ claimed responsibility for the attack. In their joint statement, they claimed that the bombing was revenge for an Israeli action, though they did not mention Sidr's name.

15. The security barrier separating Gaza and Israel was successful in halting virtually all suicide bombing infiltrations during the intifada. After the fence was rebuilt in 2001, only two suicide bombers were able to enter Israel proper via Gaza, and neither had slipped through the fence. According to Brig. Gen. Michael Herzog, the top military advisor to the Israeli defense minister during this period, a Pakistani suicide bomber with a British passport infiltrated Israel in 2003 without his explosives being detected and blew himself up at a bar. Another bomber was smuggled in a container en route to the Ashdod port in spring 2004, where he detonated himself. Neither bomber infiltrated via the fence.

16. According to Israeli Brig. Gen. Michael Herzog, "It would be a big mistake to [have] the monitoring done solely by intelligence people. The intelligence people cannot always understand the military implications of counterterror measures. Military personnel are

key. There needs to be a better integration between experts on security and experts on intelligence" (personal communication, December 22, 2004).

17. Dennis Ross, *The Missing Peace: The Inside Story of the Fight for Middle East Peace* (New York: Farrar, Straus, Giroux, 2004), pp. 770–771.

18. Greg Myre, "On the Air, Palestinians Soften Tone on Israelis," *New York Times*, December 15, 2004.

19. Ibid. In the December 3, 2004, sermon, cleric Muhammad Abu Hunud stated, "We must respect the human mind, recognize the 'other,' respect his humanity, and show tolerance to him. . . . One must not coerce. . . . Through this Islamic way of preaching, the ideas of 'the golden mean' and moderation and the avoidance of any kind of extremism or inclination to violence or fanaticism becomes ingrained in people's minds."

20. Other third-party contingents that have played a useful role in the Arab-Israeli arena are the UN Truce Supervision Organization (UNTSO) force in Jerusalem, deployed following the 1949 armistice, and the CIA observers deployed in the Mitla Pass in the aftermath of the Sinai II disengagement accord of 1975.

21. See David Makosky, "Israelis, Palestinians, and the Politics of International Military Intervention," in Robert Satloff, ed., *International Military Intervention: A Detour on the Road to Israeli-Palestinian Peace* (Washington, D.C.: The Washington Institute for Near East Policy, 2003).

22. Ahmed Aboul Gheit, joint press conference with Israeli foreign minister Silvan Shalom, Jerusalem, December 1, 2004.

23. Makosky, "Israelis, Palestinians, and the Politics of International Military Intervention." According to a 2002 study conducted by Tel Aviv University's Tami Steinmetz Center for Peace Research, 61 percent of Israelis oppose the idea of "stationing armed international policing forces that would separate between the sides and take action against anyone who used force." This finding is all the more significant because the poll was taken during a period of unrelenting terrorist attacks in Israeli urban centers, when Israelis might well have been expected to welcome any proposal that had a chance of reducing terrorism. See also Tamar Hermann and Ephraim Yuchtman-Yaar, eds., *International Intervention in Protracted Conflicts: The Israeli-Palestinian Case* (proceedings of a symposium cosponsored by the Konrad Adenauer Foundation and the Tami Steinmetz Center for Peace Research, Tel Aviv University, April 29, 2002) (Tel Aviv: Tami Steinmetz Center, 2003), p. 93.

24. Ze'ev Schiff, "PA Seals Off 12 Arms-Smuggling Tunnels in Gaza," *Haaretz* (Tel Aviv), February 25, 2005.

25. As quoted on Israel Radio, May 1, 2004.

26. According to the official disengagement plan, "The State of Israel will evacuate the Gaza Strip, including all existing Israeli towns and villages, and will redeploy outside the

Strip. This will not include military deployment in the area of the border between the Gaza Strip and Egypt ('the Philadelphia Route')."

27. Gavin Rabinowitz, "Israel Draws Up Plans to Thwart Gaza Weapons Smuggling," Associated Press, March 2, 2005.

28. In wondering whether the Philadelphia Corridor will become a rallying cry for attacks, some invoke the Shebaa Farms, a patch of borderland that Hizballah claimed for Lebanon after Israel unilaterally withdrew from that country in May 2000. Since Israel's departure, Shebaa has episodically been a flashpoint for attacks by Hizballah, which justifies its actions by claiming that Israel remains an occupier.

29. The full text of the peace treaty is available on the Multinational Force and Observers website (www.mfo.org/site_tree/54/document_library.asp).

30. It is well known that the tunnel smuggling between Egypt and Gaza is not just about arms; much of it is run by families on both sides of the border who view smuggling as part of their livelihood. Accordingly, a modicum of economic development on both the Egyptian and Palestinian sides of Rafah could help curb smuggling activity. Although economic incentives cannot solve the problem, they can be a useful component of an overall package that focuses on halting infiltration.

31. Nina Gilbert, "Mofaz: Egypt and Israel to Fight Terror Jointly," *Jerusalem Post*, December 7, 2004.

32. The issue of upgrading the Egyptian security presence near the border was discussed in high-level meetings between security personnel throughout the second half of 2004. At a December 1, 2004, joint press conference in Jerusalem with Israeli foreign minister Silvan Shalom, Egyptian foreign minister Ahmed Aboul Gheit stated, "According to the Egyptian-Israeli peace treaty, there are certain areas of limitation of forces and personnel in areas adjoining the borders." Alluding to Israel's consent to the upgrade, Gheit added that "the ability of Egyptian personnel, the police forces, to project themselves has been empowered." A transcript of the press conference was posted on the Israeli ministry of foreign affairs website (www.mfa.gov.il).

33. Gen. Omar Suleiman, interview by author, Washington, D.C., October 6, 2004.

34. Privately, Egyptian officials would prefer that the Palestinians not have a decisionmaking role in the MFO structure dealing with general Sinai-related issues. Therefore, the parties may need to consider whether the Rafah border mission should be a distinct legal entity from the existing MFO, given the need for consultations on Gaza border issues with the Palestinians.

35. Human Rights Watch, "Alternatives to House Destruction," in "The Security Situation in Rafah," chapter 4 of *Razing Rafah: Mass Home Demolitions in the Gaza Strip*, October 18, 2004. Available online (http://hrw.org/reports/2004/rafah1004/6.htm#_Toc84676187).

36. Some have suggested that commercial oil companies could also provide help with seismic technology.

37. According to Sharon's disengagement plan of June 6, 2004, "If and when conditions emerge for the evacuation of this area, Israel will be prepared to examine the possibility of establishing a seaport and an airport in the Gaza Strip, subject to arrangements that will be determined with Israel."

IMPROVING GAZA'S ECONOMIC PROSPECTS

GAZA IS IN THE MIDST OF A SERIOUS ECONOMIC CRISIS, ONE that will require creative engineering if the territory is to recuperate after Israeli withdrawal. Already in trouble before the intifada, Gaza's economy was grievously damaged by the terror and violence that erupted in 2000. Since then, Gaza's commercial links with the West Bank have been severed, and movement of agricultural and commercial goods into and out of the Strip has been seriously delayed due to Israeli closures, which are regularly instituted in response to continuing attacks.

Gaza has traditionally been an exporter of labor, but employment in Israel was curtailed for long stretches during the 1990s and virtually eliminated during much of the intifada. Palestinian unemployment increased steadily between 2000 and 2004; currently, the World Bank estimates the figure at 27 percent (35 percent in Gaza alone).[1] Real per capita income levels for the West Bank and Gaza dropped by almost 30 percent during the intifada, down to $934 per year. Gaza's dire poverty is exacerbated by its demographic growth, with a projected birthrate of 3.83 in 2004.[2] The mix of declining income and expanding population took its toll. By the end of 2004, an estimated 65 percent of Gazans and 38 percent of West Bank residents lived under the poverty line (i.e., $2.10 per day for a family of six).[3] Sixteen percent of Palestinians, mainly in Gaza, were even worse off, falling under the subsistence poverty line.[4]

The economic situation would undoubtedly be worse if donor assistance had not essentially doubled during the intifada. In 2003 international aid reached $883 million, down from a 2002 high of $1.026 billion,[5] an average of $950 million for the two years.[6] In addition to foreign donations, the economic woes have been somewhat ameliorated since 2003 by increased remittances, a modest increase in investments, and $178 million in revenue previously withheld by Israel. The net effect is that 180,000 new, mostly menial, jobs have been created in the territories since 2003, with unemployment and poverty rates declining by 5 and 4 percent, respectively.[7]

The economic crisis in Gaza has been a terrible burden to ordinary Palestinians, but a boon to Hamas,[8] whose *dawa*, or educational and social welfare network, has flourished. Hamas has used economic services to attract adherents to the Muslim Brotherhood philosophy, a phenomenon similar to that seen in many Arab countries. Working toward an economically stable Gaza therefore serves the dual objectives of alleviating a serious humanitarian crisis and weakening a terrorist organization.[9]

Israeli disengagement alone will not solve Gaza's economic problems. According to the World Bank, if withdrawal is not accompanied by measures that facilitate Palestinian economic recovery—specifically, permitting a continuous labor flow into Israel, relaxing the export-import regime at crossing points, linking Gaza and the West Bank, and easing movement restrictions in the West Bank—then little change will occur in the economic sphere. Gaza would certainly benefit from economic integration with a larger market such as Israel, both in the short and long term.[10] Once the Strip is secure and stable, additional export markets could be opened, and a reliable commercial link to the West Bank established. Moreover, if President Mahmoud Abbas is able to establish a lasting ceasefire with rejectionist groups, Israel could consider granting entry to greater numbers of Gaza and West Bank workers, thus injecting fresh money into the Palestinian economy.

This is a rosy picture, one that would be welcomed by all parties in a period of relative calm. Yet, political realities tend to cloud such visions. Israel's disengagement plan stems from a logic of separation, not integration. In the short term, then, Israel's security vision is unlikely to include a free flow of Palestinian labor over the border. Suicide bombings and Qassam rocket attacks may well remain part of the postwithdrawal landscape, so the desire to promote a Palestinian economy must be balanced with Israel's desire to protect its citizens.

Security and economic prosperity go hand in hand; one cannot endure without the other. Some would argue, therefore, that economic development is a panacea: unleash it and watch stability take hold and terrorism dissipate. According to this view, economic liberalization necessarily creates a virtuous circle. What happens if theory is not borne out by reality, though?

For example, in the interests of development, the World Bank has admonished Israel to end its closures in Palestinian areas. At the same time, it has called on the Palestinian Authority (PA) to prevent attacks that trigger such closures. Yet, what if attacks continued even after development initiatives were launched? Would continued closures be justified? Should Israel be expected to leave itself vulnerable? The World Bank avoids planning for such contingencies, knowing full well that Israeli closures would continue in the face of violence. Yet, a conflict environment is precisely the sort of situation that requires contingency thinking.

A purely developmental approach to postwithdrawal Gaza is insufficient, given that its benefits for security may not manifest themselves for some time. In contrast, an improved security environment would have an almost immediate impact on economic growth. Although the goal of economic liberalization is laudable, implementing it in postwithdrawal Gaza would require the PA to ensure that Hamas and other terrorist groups refrain from attacks—not merely disavowing them, but actually preventing them.[11] Prudence requires all parties to avoid excessive optimism; instead, they should assume that the postwithdrawal security environment will be poor—or, at best, uncertain—and craft economic policy accordingly. The following sections focus on realistic short-term economic measures for Gaza.

Institutional Reform

Several key factors will affect Gaza's economic prospects following withdrawal: job creation, foreign investment, trade facilitation, the transfer of settlement assets, donor assistance, and institutional reform. The last item is particularly important given that corruption and cronyism have long riddled the PA and contributed to the popularity of Hamas. The international community is not alone in its criticisms of such corruption; the Palestinian Legislative Council (PLC) has issued anticorruption reports since 1997. In October 2004, the PLC suspended its plenary sessions for a month in protest of Yasser Arafat's refusal to sign a law enabling the council to monitor economic reform.

Without institutional change to fight such corruption, economic improvements in Gaza will be impossible, and the prospects of foreign investment will surely decline.[12] Palestinian finance minister Salam Fayad is well aware of this fact and has been gradually increasing the transparency of the PA budget. Although his success at economic reform was mixed during Arafat's tenure, some changes did come to pass amid heavy international pressure, despite the late chairman's resistance to any dilution of his power. As mentioned previously, one such reform was the payment of salaries to Palestinian security personnel through direct deposit bank accounts instead of erratic cash payments handed out by individual commanders.

Fayad has also succeeded in establishing international audits to recover Palestinian assets abroad, as well as breaking up cement and gas monopolies. Yet, far more strenuous efforts are required to reduce corruption to a degree that will encourage competition and facilitate investment. These efforts include strengthening judicial reform (as called for in the first phase of the Roadmap), strengthening external audits, and improving the public procurement process. Such measures are favored by both the Palestinians and international institutions. Taken together, they would greatly bolster the PA's institutional accountability. Moreover, economic transparency would enhance the prospects of detecting and intercepting funds earmarked for terrorist activities—from Israel's perspective, the most important benefit.

Job Creation

Exported labor is the traditional bulwark of the Palestinian economy. In the early 1990s, the UN declared that every Palestinian who held a job in Israel could in effect feed ten Palestinians in the West Bank or Gaza. An estimated 125,000 Palestinians—many of them from Gaza—worked in Israel during that period, mostly as day laborers. The increase in suicide bombings between 1995 and 1996 triggered Israeli closures, however, making Palestinians an unreliable labor source for Israeli employers, who turned instead to imported labor from Romania, Thailand, and the Philippines. With the exception of a two-year period in the late 1990s when Palestinian attacks temporarily abated, the Israeli economy has accustomed itself to the absence, or at least rarity, of Palestinian labor. In recent years, however, Israel began to expel larger numbers of non-Palestinian foreign laborers, suggesting that its markets would be amenable to the return of Palestinian laborers if security conditions permitted.

Israeli, Palestinian, and World Bank officials have privately indicated that the number of Israeli work permits granted to Gazans is small, fluctuating between 10,000 and 15,000. After a spate of attacks in early 2004, Israeli authorities informally closed the Erez Industrial Zone, further curtailing Palestinian employment. A more useful figure is the number of "workers crossing daily," which stood at 1,000 to 4,000 in late 2004.[13] Similarly, an October 2004 World Bank report found that the number of Gazans employed in Jewish settlements and in Israel proper had decreased by 99 percent from 2000.[14] Current Israeli policy does not anticipate a reversal of this trend. Prime Minister Ariel Sharon's June 2004 disengagement plan calls for phasing out Gaza labor permits entirely by the end of 2008. That is, after all, the premise of disengagement: Israelis leave Gaza, and Gazans leave Israel.

Given this uncertain environment, it is more prudent to focus on labor-intensive capital investment and development projects inside Gaza, at least in the short and intermediate term. Infrastructure development projects, vocational training programs, and related initiatives (e.g., having Palestinians operate greenhouses formerly owned by settlers) could generate jobs and promote economic growth while minimizing risks to investors who want to help Gaza, such as the World Bank's Multilateral Investment Guarantee Agency (MIGA) and the U.S. Overseas Private Investment Corporation (OPIC).

Infrastructure Projects

Many Gaza workers have experience from Israeli construction sites and are readily available to build and repair Gaza's own infrastructure, most of which has been decimated or neglected in recent years. Saeb Bamya, director-general of the PA economics ministry, recommended that infrastructure redevelopment be the linchpin of a general economic strategy, providing both employment and the material foundation of a functioning society.[15] The Palestinians may well receive an influx of money from donor nations after the Israeli withdrawal; according to the World Bank, "It is imperative that the PA use any such windfall to create infrastructure, skills and an environment attractive to private investors."[16] Assuming annual donations of $1.5 billion, the Bank proposed that $500 million be dedicated each year to infrastructure projects. Among the Bank's recommended priority areas are repairs to the main north-south highway, new health clinics, the extension of water and electricity distribution networks, a desalination plant, sewerage, and solid-waste projects.[17]

The World Bank has a history of supporting infrastructure projects in developing countries and could establish a trust fund for this purpose in Gaza. Financing for such projects was appropriated by donor nations some time ago; it was set aside due to the intifada. For example, the $200 million that the U.S. Agency for International Development (USAID) earmarked for Palestinian infrastructure development has yet to be tapped, and Germany has reserved $125 million for the same purpose. These available funds could jumpstart infrastructure renewal in Gaza, without any delay for fundraising.

One key sector in need of development is power generation. Although Israel will continue providing electricity to Gaza under the terms of its disengagement plan (see appendix 6, part VIII), a new power plant in the Strip would help reduce Palestinian dependence on Israel. Such a plant could also export electricity to Egypt and Israel.

Water desalination is another key issue on the infrastructure agenda. The Gaza aquifer is overused, and Israel has committed to providing the Palestinians with water after disengagement. In 2003, Palestinians in Gaza used approximately 130 million cubic meters of water, well over the aquifer's sustainable yield of 96 million cubic meters.[18] (Nearly all of Gaza's aquifer lies beneath the Israeli settlement bloc of Gush Katif in the southwestern corner of the Strip; the settlers themselves used 7 to 10 million cubic meters in 2003). Palestinian resistance to a desalination project—grounded in their concern that such a project would undermine their water claims in final-status talks—has waned in recent years. In 2001, the PA welcomed a USAID initiative to build a large desalination plant in Gaza. That project stalled following Arafat's refusal to investigate the 2003 murder of three U.S. contractors in Gaza, but should be restarted. A desalination plant would provide jobs and decrease Palestinian dependence on both the Gaza aquifer and Israeli-supplied water.[19]

New Housing

With nearly 1.4 million residents, Gaza is one of the most densely populated areas on earth. Palestinians often assert that 60 percent of Gazans are refugees who, in 1948, left their homes in what is now Israel, though this figure is unconfirmed. Historically, Palestinian leaders have opposed Israeli suggestions that they build new housing in Gaza, despite the extraordinary need for it. The leadership calculated that it was preferable to leave dispossessed Palestinians in refugee camps in order to sustain their anti-Israel resentment. Ordinary Palestinians have also opposed new construction, fearing that it would undermine their case for the "right of return" to Israel proper. Their concern is well founded: Israelis across the political spectrum have long objected to any large-scale readmission of Palestinian refugees, so such a return is highly unlikely.[20]

More recently, Palestinian attitudes toward new residential construction in Gaza appear to have changed somewhat. In late 2004, then–housing minister Abdul Rahman Hamad announced that the PA hoped to build 17,000 housing units in Gaza following Israeli withdrawal.[21] In the mid-1990s, the United States, in coordination with the Palestinians, built five eight-story apartment buildings (the Karameh Towers) in Gaza. USAID abandoned further construction plans, however, amid dissatisfaction with how the PA allocated the apartments to Arafat cronies and security personnel instead of to the needy. (Subsequently, USAID created a successful small-loan program for Palestinian housing repairs and upgrades.[22]) Such experiences need not veto the idea of housing projects; rather, they show that construction programs should be carefully planned to avoid favoritism. Major residential development in Gaza would have numerous benefits (not the least of which would be employment for the many Gaza laborers with construction skills) and is certainly worth trying again.

Industrial Parks

Currently, there are two industrial parks nominally inside Gaza: the Erez Industrial Zone (EIZ) and the Gaza Industrial Estate (GIE, sometimes referred to as Karni because of its location at the Karni crossing). Before the intifada, nearly 100 Israeli companies, 98 Palestinian businesses, and 6 joint ventures were based in the EIZ, which is protected by Israeli security forces.[23] Although the zone remained open during much of the intifada, employing some 4,900 Palestinians, the violence eventually took its toll. It has been mostly dormant since January 2004, after multiple attacks, including suicide bombings, against Israelis there.[24]

Following complaints from factory owners that frequent closures were causing unsustainable economic losses, Israeli trade minister Ehud Olmert announced in June 2004 that Israel would withdraw from the EIZ as part of its Gaza disengagement. Israel then announced that it would offer grants to owners willing to relocate their factories to the peripheral Galilee and Negev areas.[25] The World Bank urged Israel to find a way to keep the zone open and leave the Israeli market open to goods manufactured there. In its June 6, 2004, disengagement plan, Sharon's cabinet recommended exploring ways to transfer ownership of the EIZ to either the Palestinians or international parties. That suggestion left open the possibility of a future trilateral industrial zone between Israel, Egypt, and the Palestinians—probably not at Erez, but rather adjacent to the Egyptian-Gaza border in the Kerem Shalom region.

In planning for the postwithdrawal environment, the World Bank favors the GIE model because, unlike Erez, it was designed to operate under Palestinian security control. Yet, that distinction also led to the GIE being nonoperational during the intifada, as Israeli businessmen feared the security situation there.

Even if the GIE is revived, and its 100 Israeli factories are sold to Palestinians, industrial parks are not a sure means of sparking quick, massive job creation. Both Palestinian and Israeli officials have expressed doubts about the World Bank's modest assertion that a revived GIE and EIZ could yield 8,500 new jobs by 2008. Certainly, they argue, it would make sense to ensure that the GIE is fully utilized and successful before creating more industrial parks in Gaza.[26] Neither would joint Palestinian-Egyptian industrial parks in Sinai solve the labor problem. The average wage in Gaza is only $250 per month, but the equivalent figure in Sinai is a third of that. Hence, there is little Palestinian motivation to seek jobs there, or Egyptian desire to employ Palestinians.

One variant on the industrial park idea that warrants exploration is a Qualifying Industrial Zone (QIZ) similar to that which has thrived in Jordan since it made peace with Israel in 1994. Under the QIZ model, if 35 percent of a given good treated in the zone has been "substantially transformed" in both Israel and Jordan, the product is awarded free-trade status by the United States. The Jordan QIZ has been an outstanding success: Jordanian exports to the United States increased from $16 million in 1998 to $927 million by the end of 2004, a staggering gain for a small economy of approximately $23 billion.[27] In addition, the QIZ employs at least 30,000 people.

Jordan's success caused Egypt—which initially opposed the QIZ idea for fear of tying its goal of free trade with the United States to Israel—to reverse its position. In December 2004, Cairo signed a trilateral trade pact with Israel and the United States that created seven QIZs throughout Egypt. The idea is so popular in Egypt that riots broke out in Ismailiya at the end of 2004 when the city was not awarded a QIZ with Israel.[28] These zones could potentially employ nearly a quarter-million Egyptians. Accordingly, planners should consider creating both a Gaza-Israel QIZ and a three-way Palestinian-Egyptian-Israeli QIZ. A chief advantage of QIZs is that they would not require an Israeli presence in Gaza, thus eliminating the security issues that plague regular industrial parks. Gaza QIZs can be established not only at the existing GIE and EIZ sites, but also at other locations.

Vocational Training

Many Palestinians, particularly in Gaza, will need additional skills training if they are to become viable employees in a revived economy. The amount of vocational training in Gaza lags far behind that seen in the West Bank. The Strip has only one government-run vocational school for each of three key sectors: industry, agriculture, and commerce. Although Gaza boasts two private law schools, it has no private vocational schools in any of the above categories. By comparison, the West Bank is home to seven industrial schools, one agricultural school, and fifty-seven schools of commerce.[29] During the intifada, the portion of PA spending dedicated to education declined significantly, from more than a fifth of the social welfare budget to just a tenth.[30] The World Bank has correctly called for donor assistance to upgrade the skills of Palestinian workers.

Welfare Assistance

Given the dire state of poverty in Gaza, elevating the standard of living must be an immediate priority. This is particularly important in light of Hamas's adeptness at exploiting poverty for its political objectives. Unfortunately, the welfare issue has bedeviled donor countries. On the one hand, they are concerned that PA spending on public sector wages has grown too quickly, and that adding expenditures for both welfare and social services might exacerbate the PA's efficiency problems. This concern reinforces the need for international oversight and transparent Palestinian institutional finances.

On the other hand, donors understand that Hamas cannot be permitted to remain a principal provider of social services. As Larry Garber, former director of USAID efforts in the West Bank and Gaza, put it, efforts must be made to "improve the quality of PA social services, on the assumption that Hamas is now competing based on quality of services provided to the population."[31] Garber correctly underscored the limitations inherent in publicly funded welfare services, adding that the international community must "recognize that the broader issue is poverty. "Unless the economy grows, and people have jobs," he concluded, "any solution will just be a Band-aid." In an encouraging sign that the PA is determined to combat Hamas's influence in this regard, the Ad Hoc Liaison Committee (AHLC), the international body responsible for coordinating aid to the Palestinians, has begun to provide Finance Minister Salam Fayad with the necessary tools to establish a PA social welfare network. To avoid corruption in this network, accounting of AHLC funds should be transparent and vigorously monitored by internationally reputable auditing firms.

Trade Facilitation

The biggest economic opportunity for Gaza lies in the transition from exporting labor to exporting goods. Exporting manufactured and agricultural goods in particular could boost employment and economic growth.

An estimated 90 percent of Palestinian trade is with Israel, and the volume of such trade has deflated during the intifada. In 2000, Palestinian exports to Israel reached $900 million, but by the third year of the intifada they had fallen to $300 million. Palestinian importation of Israeli goods—the territories are Israel's third largest export market—also suffered during this period, dropping from approximately $2.7 billion in 2000 to half that figure within three years. Half of the imports from Israel are either produced or substantially transformed in Israel, while the other half are third-country items that merely transit Israel.[32]

Given the high unemployment rate in Gaza, increased trade is the key component of any economic plan—trade with the West Bank, with Israel, and with the rest of the world. Commerce with Israel will remain particularly important after withdrawal; if correctly handled, it could help mend divisions between the two peoples. The most immediate obstacle is, as always, security. How can interested parties sharply increase trade with Gaza while simultaneously addressing Israel's security concerns? Fortunately, both sides' legitimate concerns can be addressed with an array of technological and management initiatives, including the following:

Upgrade the Karni and Erez crossings. Palestinians have long been frustrated by the trade bottleneck at the Karni crossing. The checkpoint is plagued by seemingly interminable delays lasting as long as a dozen days. Some Palestinians are convinced that the delays constitute a form of collective punishment for attempted suicide attacks against Israel. Israel denies that charge and attributes the delays to necessary security checks and the "back-to-back" unloading and reloading of trucks, required to prevent the infiltration of explosives.

Indeed, the delays are largely due to inefficient security methods, which also increase transaction costs. Although technological solutions are readily available that would streamline crossing procedures without diminishing Israel's understandably high security standards, the barrier is, again, cost. For example, shipping container scanners cost $7 million per unit.[33] Currently, Israel has only one such scanner on the ground, operable only a few hours per day at Karni. (As of this writing, Israel had recently purchased four more scanners.) The cost of procuring more scanners seems negligible relative to the level of international interest in boosting the Gaza economy, and World Bank officials believe outside donors are willing to finance such expenditures.[34]

The World Bank and Israeli officials have also indicated that Israel plans to relocate and expand the Erez terminal to its side of the border.[35] The upgraded facility will be equipped with security scanners, greatly expediting the transfer of cargo. It is slated for completion in August 2005.

Standardize operating policies at Karni and Erez. It is a truism that businesspeople crave predictability. Although Israel should never compromise its security requirements, it must realize that frequent and haphazard closing of the Karni crossing fosters instability in Gaza, which in turn threatens Israeli security. Upgrading terminal crossings could have a positive impact on the Palestinian economy in the aftermath of disengagement, since Israel will clearly remain the primary, if not sole, outlet for Palestinian goods for some time.

Toward the end of 2004, Israel signaled to the World Bank that it would now treat crossings as "normally open" instead of "normally closed." Specifically, Israel indicated that it would avoid indefinite Gaza terminal closures in the event of isolated security incidents. If security required the closing of Erez, Israel would nevertheless try to find a way to keep Karni open.[36] According to Baruch Spiegel, Israel's top security official in charge of improving humanitarian conditions for the Palestinians, biometric "smart cards" will eventually be issued to facilitate identification and quick passage, and crossings will be run by civilians, not the Israel Defense Forces.[37] Having private companies manage the terminals will necessitate the publishing of performance standards for cargo management, thereby increasing predictability.

Another idea to consider is awarding fast-track inspections to reputable manufacturers with a history of reliability and safety. Of course, the Palestinians must prevent terrorists from targeting crossings, as has all too often been the case during the intifada.

Consider a rail line between Gaza and the West Bank. Under the Oslo Accords, Israelis and Palestinians pledged to establish "safe passage" between Gaza and the West Bank, which are separated by some thirty miles. As mentioned in chapter 3, however, Israel effectively vetoed the notion of open borders following numerous suicide bomber infiltrations during the 1990s. In 2000, Prime Minister Ehud Barak openly discussed the prospect of obtaining Japanese financing for either an elevated highway or a tunnel to link the two territories. Currently, such projects seem not only prohibitively expensive, but also inordinately time-consuming, given the urgent need to improve conditions for Palestinians in Gaza as quickly as possible.[38]

A more practical solution is a rail line between the territories. Rail is an efficient way to move goods and people while maintaining reasonable security requirements. Moreover, Israel's West Bank fence, currently under construction, should allay concerns about terrorists exploiting such a route to infiltrate Israel proper. Previous discussions have anticipated a line running from Gaza to Tarkimiya, outside Hebron. After such a line is established, a feasibility study could be undertaken to determine whether automobiles could be ferried on the trains.

Upgrade Ashdod port. As discussed in chapter 3, Palestinians will remain dependent on the Israeli port of Ashdod, at least in the short term, even if they build a seaport in Gaza or gain access to the Egyptian ports of al-Arish or Said. Ashdod could serve as an additional Palestinian point of entry in the long term as well, though certain precautions must be taken to make this feasible.

First, Israel should create a rail line between the port and Erez in order to facilitate movement of goods. According to Itamar Yaar, a member of Israel's National Security Council, the 3.5 kilometers of rail needed to complete such a link (a southward rail line already exists between Ashdod and Ashkelon) should cost less than $7 million.[39] Baruch Spiegel believes Ashdod and Erez will be connected by rail before the end of 2005.[40]

Second, Israel should build a separate Palestinian pier at Ashdod, which could be symbolically monitored by a multinational force but, in practice, supervised by a professional cargo management company such as Lloyd's of London. Specialists could expedite export-import activities, requiring Israel's involvement only in the event of a security breach.

Third, Israel should build a bonded warehouse for Palestinian goods, which would help preserve perishable goods. Given the international community's stake in boosting Palestinian trade, foreign donors should help fund all of these projects.

Retain the Israeli-Palestinian customs union. Israel should reassess any intentions it may have about abrogating its customs union with Gaza following withdrawal.[41] Established in the 1994 Paris Protocols, the union delineates terms for economic relations between Israel and the PA. Both sides have reasons to preserve the agreement. It gives Palestinians preferential access to Israeli markets as well as two-thirds of revenues from imports processed by Israel and transferred to the territories. The Palestinians likely hope to maintain this arrangement in part because they will need time to get their own customs regime organized. Israel benefits from the union as well, in that it can directly deduct the cost of electricity, water, gas, fuel, telecommunications, and other Palestinian expenses. Israel also benefits from preferred access to Palestinian markets. In general, renewed Israeli and Palestinian economic talks should permit mutual adjustment to the Paris Protocols. If, after withdrawal, Israel finds that it no longer controls goods entering Rafah, it could well insist that a third party (e.g., Egypt, a multinational force, or a professional firm) enforce the customs union. Failure to find a reliable partner would invariably lead Israel to reevaluate and perhaps eliminate the union.

Accelerate tariff reduction for Palestinian products in inter-Arab trade. The 2002 Arab Summit in Beirut declared that Palestinian goods sold to Arab countries would be afforded free-trade status beginning in 2005. Egypt, Jordan, Morocco, and Tunisia have formed a free-trade area, but they have not yet incorporated the Palestinians. Such a move would undoubtedly spur Palestinian exports and should therefore be hastened.

Settlement Assets

The seventeen Israeli settlements in Gaza house about 7,000 inhabitants and take up approximately 15 to 20 percent of the territory. According to the World Bank, the settlers make little use of water or land for agriculture, employing only 3.3 square kilometers for that purpose.[42] The Palestinians could examine the prospects of increasing the agricultural output of that area following Israel's withdrawal.

More important, the World Bank has recommended that the PA be granted the option of retaining the settlements' infrastructure assets, such as schools and other public buildings.[43] Housing Minister Abdul Rahman Hamad stated that the PA would declare settlement assets public property after withdrawal, preventing their seizure by warlords.[44] There is a potential conflict here, however: Israel believes that it is entitled to compensation for public structures handed over to the PA, while the Palestinians believe it is they who are entitled to compensation for Israel's unlawful use of settlement lands. One solution to this disagreement is for Israel to invite an international valuation company to appraise the abandoned assets, with the understanding that this independent assessment will be factored into any final-status equation down the road.

The fate of abandoned housing in the settlements is an even more sensitive issue for Israelis and Palestinians, with mixed feelings on both sides. Privately, Israeli officials have expressed concern that any images of Israel destroying such housing would be perceived as churlishness on their part, undermining the message of withdrawal as a harbinger of peace. As of March 2005, this view seemed dominant among Israeli officials.[45] (Some have ascribed such concerns and related decisionmaking to the so-called "CNN effect.") At the same time, many Israelis are concerned that residential assets handed over to the PA may be looted or allocated only to those Palestinians with political connections. Israel also fears that scenes of Hamas taking over abandoned homes or synagogues could traumatize the public and psychologically impede future withdrawals. In fact, such concerns led Israel to declare in mid-2004 that it was planning to demolish settler housing.

For their part, although the Palestinians see the value of inheriting free housing, they also realize that settler homes may be unsuited to their need for high-rise construction in densely populated areas. According to Housing Minister Hamad, the settlements' suburban-style homes do not meet the Palestinians' more pressing need for public housing; in late 2004, he announced that Saudi Arabia and the United Arab Emirates were willing to provide some financial assistance for the construction of 1,500 multi-family units to replace existing single-family housing.[46] Israel is probably amenable to demolishing the houses it abandons to facilitate such a plan, but seems to be waiting for an official PA request in order to avoid negative publicity in the eyes of the international community.[47]

Given the politically charged nature of the disposal of settlement assets, the AHLC and the World Bank should help the PA with the transfer process in order to provide oversight and prevent cronyism. Although neither body would likely accept formal custodianship, they can both provide a template for efficient oversight and establish a transparent claims process.

In addition, the PA may need to establish a new agency to assist in the transfer and adjudicate conflicting land claims. Such rival claims may emerge despite the generally accepted convention that 90 to 95 percent of the Israeli settlements in Gaza were built on land that has been public property since the Ottoman era.[48] In general, the highly charged question of which settlement assets should remain standing requires Israeli-Palestinian coordination well in advance of the pullout.

International Donor Assistance

During the intifada, international donors contributed approximately $950 million annually ($310 per capita per year) to help the Palestinian economy, making it one of the most well-supported developing economies in the world.[49] Outgoing World Bank president James Wolfensohn has suggested increasing foreign donations by 50 percent, or $500 million, predicated on expanded Israeli-Palestinian economic and security cooperation.[50] Such an increase would boost per capita assistance in the West Bank and Gaza to $380 per year, generating a 26 percent increase in gross domestic product in 2006 and decreasing unemployment close to the pre-intifada level of 14 percent. Poverty levels would also shrink, though still remain high.[51]

Much of this extra funding could come from Arab states. In the final communiqué of the 2002 Arab Summit, member states pledged to provide $55 million per month in fiscal support to the PA through the end of the intifada.[52] Yet, data published by the Palestinian finance ministry in early 2005 indicated that only about $9 million of this monthly assistance was actually reaching the PA.[53] Of this amount, $7 million came from Saudi Arabia, which gained a massive $31 *billion* windfall in oil revenues in 2003 alone. Collectively, Arab countries that had promised aid to the Palestinians fell short by $46 million per month, or $552 million yearly. Citing internal data from the International Monetary Fund and the PA, U.S. officials recently asserted that Arab League states owed the PA $891.8 million.[54]

At a December 2004 AHLC meeting in Oslo, donor countries endorsed the World Bank's conditional funding recommendations. Specifically, the World Bank hopes that, by withholding the $500 million in extra funds, it can convince Israel to lift closures and persuade Palestinians to improve their security apparatus. The current AHLC position is to monitor the situation and review its own stance accordingly. Yet, its December meeting occurred before Abbas was elected. Abbas's subsequent commitments to security reform, as well as Israel's commitment to improving Palestinian quality of life, seem to have had an impact. At a March 1, 2005, London conference hosted by British prime minister Tony Blair and attended by a wide array of foreign ministers (including Secretary of State Condoleezza Rice), donor countries pledged $1.2 billion to assist the Palestinians in 2005.[55]

Revived Multilateral Talks

The Quartet, and Arab states in particular, could reinforce peacemaking by reviving the multilateral talks of the 1990s. Those talks focused on a variety of largely economic projects, many of which could benefit the entire region. Among the topics covered were economic development, water rights, environmental issues, arms control, and refugees. While progress on these issues may vary (with discussion of non-economic issues likely to reap only modest rewards, in anticipation of eventual final-status negotiations), such talks would be useful in acclimating regional players to looking beyond the territorial issues of the Israeli-Palestinian conflict and considering broader regional change. The mere existence of such negotiations would send a message of fresh hope to the peoples of the Middle East.

Notes

1. World Bank, *Stagnation or Revival? Israeli Disengagement and Palestinian Economic Prospects*, December 2, 2004, pp. 3, 7. According to an earlier World Bank report, the number of unemployed Gazans reached a high of 46 percent in 2002 (*Disengagement, the Palestinian Economy, and the Settlements*, June 23, 2004, p. 31). The Palestinian economy stabilized in 2003 and even experienced an estimated 6 percent growth rate. Even so, 70 percent of new Gaza entrants to the job market could not find a job, 43 percent of Gaza males between the ages of fifteen and twenty-four were unemployed, and the growth rate was actually only 1 percent per capita.

2. "The Gaza Strip," *CIA World Factbook*, accessed online January 3, 2005 (www.cia.gov/cia/publications/factbook/geos/gz.html).

3. World Bank, *Stagnation or Revival?* pp. 3, 7.

4. Ibid., pp. 32–33.

5. Ibid., p. 64.

6. Ibid., p. 3.

7. Ibid., p. 6.

8. Matthew Levitt, *Exposing Hamas: Funding Terror under the Cover of Charity* (New Haven: Yale University Press, forthcoming in 2005).

9. See David Makovsky, "A Multi-Prong Strategy to Defeat Hamas," *International Herald Tribune*, March 1, 2005.

10. Egypt, another large neighboring market, has not been receptive to Palestinian goods.

11. According to a poll conducted by the Ramallah-based Palestinian Center for Policy and Survey Research in December 2004, Palestinian support for attacks in Israel dropped from 54 percent (in September 2003) to 49 percent, while 82 percent indicated that they would support a ceasefire. In addition, 54 percent stated that all attacks from Gaza should stop in the event of an Israeli withdrawal. These positive trends will hopefully allow Abbas to act against militants. Khalil Shikaki, "Public Opinion Poll #14: Results," Palestinian Center for Policy and Survey Research, December 1–5, 2004. Available online (www.pcpsr.org/survey/polls/2004/p14a.html#support).

12. In June 2004, Nigel Roberts, World Bank director for the West Bank and Gaza, stated, "Palestinian reforms need to go beyond security," adding that the PA must "create a more attractive environment for the private sector." Sophi Claudet, "Gaza Pullout to Succeed Only If Israel Opens Border: World Bank," Agence France Presse, June 29, 2004.

13. Author interviews with Col. Amiram Vardi (Israel Defense Forces, chief economic advisor), August 15, 2004, and Nigel Roberts (World Bank director for the West Bank and Gaza), October 6, 2004.

14. World Bank, *Four Years—Intifada, Closures, and Palestinian Economic Crisis: An Assessment*, October 2004, p. 4. Available online (http://siteresources.worldbank.org/INTWESTBANKGAZA/Resources/wbgaza-4yrassessment.pdf).

15. In a report entitled "Building the State of Palestine: The Process of Achieving Economic Viability" (submitted to the UN Conference on Trade and Development, Sao Paulo, Brazil, June 13–18, 2004), Bamya wrote: "Job creation programs in the emergency period must be geared towards buttressing the survival of the private sector and the creation of the needed infrastructure (construction) for the enhancement of trade capabilities in the future. Such projects as roads rehabilitation, the rebuilding of the Gaza airport and sea port, as well as liquid and solid waste treatment facilities are of the utmost importance in this employment generation concept."

16. World Bank, *Disengagement, the Palestinian Economy, and the Settlements*, p. 8.

17. Ibid., p. 11.

18. Ibid., p. 14.

19. On January 13, 2005, in the immediate aftermath of Abbas's electoral victory, USAID announced that it would finance the construction of an emergency pipeline to bring fresh water to 150,000 residents of Gaza. The project will connect Israel's Mekorot pipeline (at Nahal Oz, just north of Gaza) to the Gaza City reservoir, servicing the eastern portion of Gaza City. The extended pipeline will measure nearly 12 kilometers: 9 kilometers in Israel and 2.7 in Gaza. USAID will finance the Gaza portion. Once activated, the pipeline will deliver five million cubic meters of water annually. UN Information System on the Question of Palestine, "OPT: USAID Brings Water to 150,000 Gazans," January 12, 2005. Available online (http://domino.un.org/UNISPAL.NSF/0/5532af54a4cf7ec685256f88005210a2?OpenDocument).

20. Even some Palestinians have come to realize that a mass migration of refugees into Israel is no longer realistic. During a June 15, 2004, interview with Israel Radio, Jibril Rajoub, head of the Palestinian National Security Council, stated that the Palestinians cannot change the Jewish demographic character of Israel. Similarly, Palestinian intellectual Sari Nusseibeh collected 150,000 Palestinian signatures calling for a peace plan that disavows the right of return. Following a survey conducted in summer 2003, Palestinian pollster Khalil Shikaki claimed that fewer Palestinians would seek to fulfill that right than previously thought ("Results of PSR Refugees' Polls in the West Bank/Gaza Strip, Jordan, and Lebanon on Refugees' Preferences and Behavior in a Palestinian-Israeli Permanent Refugee Agreement," Palestinian Center for Policy and Survey Research, July 18, 2003; available online at www.pcpsr.org/survey/polls/2003/refugeesjune03.html). Given these views, the Palestinians should review their past opposition to Gaza construction and embark on housing a needy population.

21. Khaled Abu Toameh, "PA Prepares Plan for Gaza Takeover," *Jerusalem Post*, December 20, 2004.

22. Larry Garber (former USAID director for the West Bank and Gaza), interview by author, December 3, 2004.

23. Figures obtained from the Israeli ministry of trade and industry in 2004.

24. According to Itzik Amitay, the EIZ's general manager, "Few if any of the Jewish owners show up anymore. They feel it is simply too dangerous." Matthew Gutman, "Erez Zone to Be Trial for Gaza Withdrawal," *Jerusalem Post*, July 29, 2004.

25. "Solution for Factories Moved from Erez: New Industrial Zone near Rafah," *Maariv* (Asaqim supplement), July 18, 2004.

26. World Bank, *Stagnation or Revival?* p. 6. Information also obtained from author interviews with Saeb Bamya, director-general of the PA economics ministry, and Gabi Bar, director of the Israeli ministry of trade and industry's international division, August 2004.

27. Information obtained from the Jordanian government in 2004 and from the 2003 *CIA World Factbook*.

28. See Thomas Friedman, "New Signs on the Arab Street," *New York Times*, March 13, 2005.

29. Information obtained from the website of the PA ministry of education and higher education (www.mohe.gov.ps/English).

30. Information obtained from the 2003–2004 monthly reports of the PA ministry of finance. Available online (www.mof.gov.ps/Reports-E.htm).

31. Larry Garber, interview by author, December 9, 2004.

32. Gabi Bar (director, Israeli ministry of trade and industry, international division), interview by author, August 17, 2004.

33. Boaz Radai (economic attaché, Israeli embassy, Washington, D.C.), interview by author, July 23, 2004.

34. Markus Kostner (World Bank official), interview by author, December 11, 2004.

35. World Bank, *Stagnation or Revival?* p. 10.

36. Ibid., p. 12.

37. Interview by author, January 31, 2005.

38. Dennis Ross, former U.S. peace envoy, stated that the United States had planned to finance such a project as part of the Camp David accords in July 2000 (personal communication, October 2004).

39. Dan Gerstenfield, "Train May Connect Gaza to Ashdod," *Jerusalem Post,* October 20, 2004.

40. Interview by author, January 31, 2005.

41. World Bank, *Stagnation or Revival?* p. 1.

42. World Bank, *Disengagement, the Palestinian Economy, and the Settlements,* p. 14.

43. World Bank, *Stagnation or Revival?* p. 23.

44. Abu Toameh, "PA Prepares Plan for Gaza Takeover."

45. In a February 28, 2005, interview on Israel Radio, Israeli national security advisor Gen. Giora Eiland stated, "We advise against destroying the homes. . . . When you weigh the pros and cons . . . it would be better to try to reach agreement to hand over the houses in an organized manner . . . to international or more responsible Palestinian parties." In an April 13 interview with CNN's Wolf Blitzer, Ariel Sharon stated that he did not want to destroy such buildings, and that he could convince the cabinet to back his view.

46. Abu Toameh, "PA Prepares Plan for Gaza Takeover." Hamad stated, "We have a plan to build 17,000 homes there to help solve the severe housing crisis in the Gaza Strip."

47. One interesting alternative plan for assets transfer was scuttled in February 2005 amid negative publicity. Muhammad al-Bar, a Gulf businessman, met with Sharon and offered $56 million to purchase settler homes. See "UAE Billionaire Seeks in Vain to Buy Settler Homes in Gaza Strip," Agence France Presse, February 17, 2005.

48. World Bank, *Stagnation or Revival?* p. 17.

49. Ibid., p. ii.

50. World Bank, *Disengagement, the Palestinian Economy, and the Settlements*, foreword.

51. Ibid., p. 8.

52. According to a full summary of the communiqué prepared by *Ain-al-yaqeen.com*, April 5, 2002. Available online (www.ain-al-yaqeen.com/issues/20020405/feat6en.htm).

53. Glenn Kessler, "US to Press Arab Nations to Pay Pledges Made to Palestinians," *Washington Post*, February 26, 2005.

54. Ibid.

55. Laura Sukhtan, "Palestinian Finance Minister Says Donors Promising $1.2 Billion in 2005," Associated Press, March 1, 2005.

RECOMMENDATIONS
FOR U.S. ACTION

THE NEXT YEAR WILL BE A SIGNAL PERIOD FOR THE ISRAELI-Palestinian arena and related U.S. policy. As this study has sought to make clear, the stakes have rarely been higher, and failure or inaction will carry severe consequences. President George W. Bush will seek to prioritize his many foreign policy objectives as his second term unfolds, both within the Middle East and elsewhere. The future of Iraq and the nuclear ambitions of Iran are clearly high-priority issues, as are the wider war on terror and the advance of democratization. The administration should recognize that success on the Israeli-Palestinian front could bolster U.S. efforts to address these other crucial issues. Conversely, if the situation in Iraq worsens, the specter of a perceived U.S. defeat would undoubtedly embolden rejectionists bent on torpedoing progress in the Israeli-Palestinian arena.

The United States has a full Middle East agenda and cannot focus solely on Israel and the Palestinian Authority (PA). Nevertheless, it can capitalize on the momentum and optimism of the post-Arafat era by taking measured and determined steps to ensure continued progress. Following are nine action items that Washington should implement in the coming months.

1. Ensure a viable ceasefire and facilitate security cooperation. Washington has already dispatched Army general William "Kip" Ward to the region to restructure the Palestinian security services and revive security cooperation. Toward that end, he and his staff of twenty should work to make current ceasefire terms more precise than those of the 2003 truce, in order to avoid the problems that led to the collapse of that agreement. The United States should then monitor the ceasefire and ensure that its terms are implemented and enforced.

In addition, security coordination, both trilateral and bilateral, would have multiple benefits for Israelis and Palestinians. Security is the cornerstone of coexistence, and sustained cooperation would help rebuild trust between the two parties. Most important, such coordination would facilitate a successful withdrawal from Gaza. An improved security environment would also ameliorate conditions on the ground for Palestinians by reducing the need for Israeli checkpoints in the West Bank. Israeli defense minister Shaul Mofaz has stated that Israel is willing to pull out of major West Bank cities as soon as the PA is able to accept responsibility for controlling these areas.

2. Reactivate the Roadmap. The Roadmap is the only framework that has the support of Israel, the Palestinians, and the international community. Reactivating it would ease the suspicions of those who fear that Israel's "Gaza First" plan is actually "Gaza Only." Moreover, the new PA leadership is already undertaking Roadmap-mandated reforms toward democratization and the elimination of incitement. The PA can reinforce these reforms by reviewing its educational curriculum and removing imams who deliver incendiary sermons. For its part, Israel should honor its commitment under the Roadmap to remove roadblocks in the West Bank.

3. Bridge gaps in Gaza coordination. Since Yasser Arafat's death, Israeli prime minister Sharon has indicated a willingness to coordinate the Gaza pullout with the Palestinians. A coordinated withdrawal is more likely to facilitate a smooth transfer of authority than a unilateral pullout. It could also mend badly frayed trust between the two sides and enable the continuation of the peace process. U.S. help is essential to any such effort; a coordinated disengagement of this nature requires intensive planning and management. Moreover, in order to avoid destabilization after withdrawal, the PA must commit itself to the specific terms of the disengagement.

4. Help defray the security costs of disengagement. In order to promote future withdrawals, the United States should consider helping Israel defray the military costs of the Gaza disengagement. This does not include costs associated with the evacuation of settlements; because the United States has been an unequivocal opponent of Israel's settlement policy, no American assistance in this regard is expected or necessary.

In addition, President Bush's February 2005 call for $350 million in U.S. assistance to the PA could reduce the security costs of disengagement for the Palestinians. With such funding—though without public fanfare—the United States could help the PA reform and restructure its security services as they prepare to assume responsibility for Gaza. Washington should also consider renewing its past practice of training select PA security officials in the United States.

5. Configure a multinational force for deployment on the Egyptian side of the Gaza border. The United States should help configure a multilateral force that can work with the upgraded 750-member Egyptian border police contingent to prevent weapons smuggling through tunnels dug between Sinai and Gaza. This force could be an extension of the existing Multinational Force and Observers (MFO) in Sinai. The advantage of the MFO solution is that its institutional mechanisms are already in place, saving the time and resources required to create an entirely new entity. (It may be necessary, however, to make the Gaza arm of the MFO a separate legal entity; the PA will be included in consultations on Gaza border issues, and Egypt would prefer not to give the Palestinians a decisionmaking role in a force that deals with Sinai-related issues as well.) Drawing troops from existing MFO units may not be feasible, given that their duties are different from those required at the Gaza border. Instead, various countries could contribute additional troops to form a new Gaza arm of the MFO. Although the expanded MFO would remain under U.S. leadership, most of the new troops could come from other nations. Moreover, if an MFO deployment on the Egyptian side of Rafah succeeded, it could spur similar deployments to a future Gaza seaport and airport.

6. Support sound economic policies for a postwithdrawal Gaza. The United States should continue to work closely with the World Bank on a number of Palestinian funding and employment issues, including institutional reform, infrastructure enhancement, construction projects, industrial parks, donor assistance, the disposition of settlement assets, and upgrades at the Karni crossing. Washington also has a variety of tools to foster economic development. For example, risk insurance issued by the U.S. Overseas Private Investment Corporation (OPIC) could encourage foreign investment in Gaza and should therefore be examined further. In addition, Washington should encourage Israel to give the Palestinians a pier at the Ashdod port in order to expedite Gaza trade until security issues permit some other arrangement.

At the same time, the United States and the international community should help Palestinian president Mahmoud Abbas compete with rejectionists in the provision of social services. This would help blunt the rejectionists' appeal as they enter the political arena. Hamas swept local Gaza elections in January 2005 due in large part to its track record of providing healthcare, education, and other essential services that the government had failed to deliver. Accordingly, the PA must be capable of supporting both private and public entities that can replace Hamas as providers of such services.

Clear economic improvements would also help Abbas demonstrate the financial benefits of nonviolence and reduce corruption in the mainstream Fatah Party. The latter measure is essential if Fatah is to field candidates who can defeat Hamas in future elections.

7. Urge Arab states to help the Palestinians and facilitate the peace process. The United States should urge Arab states to advance the cause of peace in three ways. First, these states should publicly condemn suicide attacks under all circumstances, making clear that such "martyrdom" operations are both morally wrong and politically counterproductive to the goal of establishing a Palestinian state. Such a pan-Arab decree would make it easier for the PA to combat terrorism.

Second, Persian Gulf states in particular can be instrumental in helping the PA and, in turn, weakening Hamas. Arab states have given the PA an estimated $891.8 million less than they pledged over the past few years, despite the doubling of oil prices. By making good on their financial commitments, these states could demonstrate that Arab support for the Palestinians is more than just a rhetorical weapon against Israel.

Third, Arab states can give Israel incentives to take more conciliatory steps toward the Palestinians by putting forward an "Arab Roadmap." Such a document would link Israeli-Palestinian progress with increased Arab-Israeli normalization, easing Israeli fears that territorial withdrawal means greater vulnerability.

8. Use leverage against rejectionists. The United States should work with the PA, Israel, Egypt, and members of the Quartet to ensure that terrorists do not undermine the disengagement. Initially, some rejectionist groups may tread carefully out of a belief that the Palestinian public is tired of violence. Yet, Hamas, Palestinian Islamic Jihad, and Hizballah will likely remain disruptive forces, actively opposing any effort to foster Israeli-Palestinian coexistence. Confrontation with terrorist groups in Gaza need not be massive in order to be effective, however. Washington should encourage Abbas to take incremental-yet-potent steps such as closing rocket workshops, arresting key operatives, and, again, removing inflammatory imams from their posts. Apart from these and other security measures, Washington should consult with the PA about how best to mobilize the Palestinian public against terrorists. Now that he has a mandate, Abbas should be encouraged to continue the effort he began on the campaign trail: namely, conditioning Palestinian societal discourse against suicide bombing.

In addition, Quartet members should leverage their ties with Iran, which backs all three of the aforementioned terrorist groups to varying degrees. Tehran's support for such groups should be raised in all European consultations with Iran. Syria, too, plays host to terrorist groups and allows its main airport to be used as a transit point for weaponry. Such activity should be a central component of bilateral and multilateral dialogue with Damascus as well.

9. Put forward a new UN Security Council resolution ratifying Gaza withdrawal.

The United States should make certain that Israel's disengagement wins not only the support of regional parties, but also formal certification from the UN Security Council. A Security Council resolution ratifying the disengagement would ensure that the terms of departure are upheld and would make the PA formally responsible for areas from which Israel withdraws. In addition, such a resolution should affirm that Resolutions 242 and 338 have been fulfilled with regard to Gaza; declare that the withdrawal is generally consistent with hopes for a two-state solution; denounce further violence; make clear that all militias must disband and submit their weapons to the PA; and affirm that, in keeping with the UN Charter, Israel has the right to self-defense if such groups continue to menace it. The existence of an internationally respected resolution drafted along these lines would give Israel strong incentive to continue the peace process.

APPENDICES

APPENDIX 1

Excerpts from Prime Minister Ariel Sharon's Speech at the Fourth Herzliya Conference, December 18, 2003

". . . We wish to speedily advance implementation of the Roadmap towards quiet and a genuine peace. We hope that the Palestinian Authority will carry out its part. However, if in a few months the Palestinians still continue to disregard their part in implementing the Roadmap, then Israel will initiate the unilateral security step of disengagement from the Palestinians.

"The purpose of the disengagement plan is to reduce terror as much as possible, and grant Israeli citizens the maximum level of security. The process of disengagement will lead to an improvement in the quality of life, and will help strengthen the Israeli economy. The unilateral steps which Israel will take in the framework of the disengagement plan will be fully coordinated with the United States. We must not harm our strategic coordination with the United States. These steps will increase security for the residents of Israel and relieve the pressure on the [Israel Defense Forces (IDF)] and security forces in fulfilling the difficult tasks they are faced with. The disengagement plan is meant to grant maximum security and minimize friction between Israelis and Palestinians.

"We are interested in conducting direct negotiations, but do not intend to hold Israeli society hostage in the hands of the Palestinians. I have already said we will not wait for them indefinitely.

"The disengagement plan will include the redeployment of IDF forces along new security lines and a change in the deployment of settlements, which will reduce as much as possible the number of Israelis located in the heart of the Palestinian population. We will draw provisional security lines, and the IDF will be deployed along them. Security will be provided by IDF deployment, the security fence, and other physical obstacles. . . .

"[R]eduction of friction will require the extremely difficult step of changing the deployment of some of the settlements. I would like to repeat what I have said in the past: in the framework of a future agreement, Israel

Source: Office of the Prime Minister, Israel

81

will not remain in all the places where it is today. The relocation of settlements will be made, first and foremost, in order to draw the most efficient security line possible, thereby creating this disengagement between Israel and the Palestinians. This security line will not constitute the permanent border of the state of Israel; however, as long as implementation of the Roadmap is not resumed, the IDF will be deployed along that line. Settlements which will be relocated are those which will not be included in the territory of the state of Israel in the framework of any possible future permanent agreement. At the same time, in the framework of the disengagement plan, Israel will strengthen its control over those same areas in the Land of Israel which will constitute an inseparable part of the state of Israel in any future agreement. I know you would like to hear names, but we should leave something for later.

"Israel will greatly accelerate the construction of the security fence. Today we can already see it taking shape. The rapid completion of the security fence will enable the IDF to remove roadblocks and ease the daily lives of the Palestinian population not involved in terror.

"In order to enable the Palestinians to develop their economic and trade sectors, and to ensure that they will not be exclusively dependent on Israel, we will consider, in the framework of the disengagement plan, enabling in coordination with Jordan and Egypt the freer passage of people and goods through international border crossings, while taking the necessary security precautions.

"I would like to emphasize: the disengagement plan is a security measure and not a political one. The steps which will be taken will not change the political reality between Israel and the Palestinians, and will not prevent the possibility of returning to the implementation of the Roadmap and reaching an agreed settlement. . . . Rather, it is a step Israel will take in the absence of any other option, in order to improve its security. The disengagement plan will be realized only in the event that the Palestinians continue to drag their feet and postpone implementation of the Roadmap. Obviously, through the disengagement plan the Palestinians will receive much less than they would have received through direct negotiations as set out in the Roadmap.

"According to circumstances, it is possible that parts of the disengagement plan that are supposed to provide maximum security to the citizens of Israel will be undertaken while also attempting to implement the Roadmap. . . ."

APPENDIX 2

Excerpts from Bush-Blair Press Conference, November 12, 2004

President George W. Bush: "... Prime Minister Blair and I also share a vision of a free, peaceful, [and] democratic broader Middle East. That vision must include a just and peaceful resolution of the Arab-Israeli conflict based on two democratic states—Israel and Palestine—living side by side in peace and security.

"Our sympathies are with the Palestinian people as they begin a period of mourning. Yet, the months ahead offer a new opportunity to make progress toward a lasting peace. Soon Palestinians will choose a new president. This is the first step in creating lasting democratic political institutions through which a free Palestinian people will elect local and national leaders.

"We're committed to the success of these elections, and we stand ready to help. We look forward to working with a Palestinian leadership that is committed to fighting terror and committed to the cause of democratic reform. We'll mobilize the international community to help revive the Palestinian economy, to build up Palestinian security institutions to fight terror, to help the Palestinian government fight corruption, and to reform the Palestinian political system and build democratic institutions.

"We'll also work with Israeli and Palestinian leaders to complete the disengagement plan from Gaza and part of the West Bank. These steps, if successful, will lay the foundation for progress in implementing the Roadmap, and then lead to final-status negotiations.

"We seek a democratic, independent, and viable state for the Palestinian people. We are committed to the security of Israel as a Jewish state. These objectives—two states living side by side in peace and security—can be reached by only one path: the path of democracy, reform, and the rule of law...."

Prime Minister Tony Blair: "... As the president rightly said, ... we meet at a crucial time where it is important that we revitalize and reinvigorate the

Source: "President and Prime Minister Blair Discussed Iraq, Middle East," transcript of White House press conference, Washington, D.C., November 12, 2004. Available online (www.whitehouse.gov/news/releases/2004/11/20041112-5.html).

search for a genuine, lasting, and just peace in the Middle East. I would like to repeat my condolences to the Palestinian people at this time.

"As you will have seen, we have set out the steps that we believe are necessary to get into a process that will lead to the two-state solution that we want to see. And I think those steps are very clear. They are, first of all, making sure that we set out a clear vision—that clear vision was articulated by President Bush some time ago, repeated by him today—of a two-state solution, two democratic states living side-by-side together in peace.

"The second thing is, we need to support those Palestinian elections. That is a chance for the first beginnings of democracy to take hold on the Palestinian side. So it's important that we support it. Thirdly, however, if we want a viable Palestinian state, we need to make sure that the political, the economic, and the security infrastructure of that state is shaped and helped to come into being. We will mobilize international opinion and the international community in order to do that.

"The fourth thing is that Prime Minister Sharon's plan for disengagement is important. I think we recognized that when we were here at the White House back in April of this year. That disengagement plan is now going forward. It's important that we support it. And then, on the basis of this, we are able, in accordance with the principles of the Roadmap, to get back into final-status negotiation, so that we have that two-state solution. And I think there is every possibility that we can do this, with the energy and the will and the recognition that, in the end, it is only if the two states that we want to see living side by side are indeed democratic states where the rule of law and human rights are respected in each of them, that a just peace could be secured...."

APPENDIX 3

Text of the Quartet Roadmap

The following is a performance-based and goal-driven roadmap, with clear phases, timelines, target dates, and benchmarks aiming at progress through reciprocal steps by the two parties in the political, security, economic, humanitarian, and institution-building fields, under the auspices of the Quartet (the United States, European Union, United Nations, and Russia). The destination is a final and comprehensive settlement of the Israel-Palestinian conflict by 2005, as presented in President Bush's speech of 24 June, and welcomed by the EU, Russia, and the UN in the 16 July and 17 September Quartet Ministerial statements.

A two-state solution to the Israeli-Palestinian conflict will only be achieved through an end to violence and terrorism, when the Palestinian people have a leadership acting decisively against terror and willing and able to build a practicing democracy based on tolerance and liberty, and through Israel's readiness to do what is necessary for a democratic Palestinian state to be established, and a clear, unambiguous acceptance by both parties of the goal of a negotiated settlement as described below. The Quartet will assist and facilitate implementation of the plan, starting in Phase I, including direct discussions between the parties as required. The plan establishes a realistic timeline for implementation. However, as a performance-based plan, progress will require and depend upon the good faith efforts of the parties, and their compliance with each of the obligations outlined below. Should the parties perform their obligations rapidly, progress within and through the phases may come sooner than indicated in the plan. Non-compliance with obligations will impede progress.

A settlement, negotiated between the parties, will result in the emergence of an independent, democratic, and viable Palestinian state living side by side in peace and security with Israel and its other neighbors. The settlement will resolve the Israel-Palestinian conflict and end the occupation that began in 1967, based on the foundations of the Madrid Confer-

Source: "A Performance-Based Roadmap to a Permanent Two-State Solution to the Israeli-Palestinian Conflict," U.S. Department of State, April 30, 2003.

ence, the principle of land for peace, UNSCRs 242, 338, and 1397, agreements previously reached by the parties, and the initiative of Saudi Crown Prince Abdullah—endorsed by the Beirut Arab League Summit—calling for acceptance of Israel as a neighbor living in peace and security, in the context of a comprehensive settlement. This initiative is a vital element of international efforts to promote a comprehensive peace on all tracks, including the Syrian-Israeli and Lebanese-Israeli tracks.

The Quartet will meet regularly at senior levels to evaluate the parties' performance on implementation of the plan. In each phase, the parties are expected to perform their obligations in parallel, unless otherwise indicated.

Phase I: Ending Terror and Violence, Normalizing Palestinian Life, and Building Palestinian Institutions, Present to May 2003

In Phase I, the Palestinians immediately undertake an unconditional cessation of violence according to the steps outlined below; such action should be accompanied by supportive measures undertaken by Israel. Palestinians and Israelis resume security cooperation based on the Tenet work plan to end violence, terrorism, and incitement through restructured and effective Palestinian security services. Palestinians undertake comprehensive political reform in preparation for statehood, including drafting a Palestinian constitution, and free, fair, and open elections upon the basis of those measures. Israel takes all necessary steps to help normalize Palestinian life. Israel withdraws from Palestinian areas occupied from September 28, 2000, and the two sides restore the status quo that existed at that time, as security performance and cooperation progress. Israel also freezes all settlement activity, consistent with the Mitchell Report.

At the outset of Phase I:

- Palestinian leadership issues unequivocal statement reiterating Israel's right to exist in peace and security and calling for an immediate and unconditional ceasefire to end armed activity and all acts of violence against Israelis anywhere. All official Palestinian institutions end incitement against Israel.

- Israeli leadership issues unequivocal statement affirming its commitment to the two-state vision of an independent, viable, sovereign Palestinian state living in peace and security alongside Israel, as expressed by President Bush, and calling for an immediate end to violence against Palestinians everywhere. All official Israeli institutions end incitement against Palestinians.

Security

- Palestinians declare an unequivocal end to violence and terrorism and undertake visible efforts on the ground to arrest, disrupt, and restrain individuals and groups conducting and planning violent attacks on Israelis anywhere.

- Rebuilt and refocused Palestinian Authority security apparatus begins sustained, targeted, and effective operations aimed at confronting all those engaged in terror and dismantlement of terrorist capabilities and infrastructure. This includes commencing confiscation of illegal weapons and consolidation of security authority, free of association with terror and corruption.

- [The government of Israel (GOI)] takes no actions undermining trust, including deportations; attacks on civilians; confiscation and/or demolition of Palestinian homes and property, as a punitive measure or to facilitate Israeli construction; destruction of Palestinian institutions and infrastructure; and other measures specified in the Tenet work plan.

- Relying on existing mechanisms and on-the-ground resources, Quartet representatives begin informal monitoring and consult with the parties on establishment of a formal monitoring mechanism and its implementation.

- Implementation, as previously agreed, of U.S. rebuilding, training, and resumed security cooperation plan in collaboration with outside oversight board (U.S.-Egypt-Jordan). Quartet support for efforts to achieve a lasting, comprehensive ceasefire.

- All Palestinian security organizations are consolidated into three services reporting to an empowered Interior Minister.

- Restructured/retrained Palestinian security forces and [Israel Defense Forces (IDF)] counterparts progressively resume security cooperation and other undertakings in implementation of the Tenet work plan, including regular senior-level meetings, with the participation of U.S. security officials.

- Arab states cut off public and private funding and all other forms of support for groups supporting and engaging in violence and terror.

- All donors providing budgetary support for the Palestinians channel these funds through the Palestinian Ministry of Finance's Single Treasury Account.

- As comprehensive security performance moves forward, IDF withdraws progressively from areas occupied since September 28, 2000, and the two sides restore the status quo that existed prior to September 28, 2000. Palestinian security forces redeploy to areas vacated by IDF.

Palestinian Institution-Building

- Immediate action on credible process to produce draft constitution for Palestinian statehood. As rapidly as possible, constitutional committee circulates draft Palestinian constitution, based on strong parliamentary democracy and cabinet with empowered prime minister, for public comment/debate. Constitutional committee proposes draft document for submission after elections for approval by appropriate Palestinian institutions.

- Appointment of interim prime minister or cabinet with empowered executive authority/decision-making body.

- GOI fully facilitates travel of Palestinian officials for [Palestinian Legislative Council (PLC)] and cabinet sessions, internationally supervised security retraining, electoral and other reform activity, and other supportive measures related to the reform efforts.

- Continued appointment of Palestinian ministers empowered to undertake fundamental reform. Completion of further steps to achieve genuine separation of powers, including any necessary Palestinian legal reforms for this purpose.

- Establishment of independent Palestinian election commission. PLC reviews and revises election law.

- Palestinian performance on judicial, administrative, and economic benchmarks, as established by the International Task Force on Palestinian Reform.

- As early as possible, and based upon the above measures and in the context of open debate and transparent candidate selection/electoral campaign based on a free, multi-party process, Palestinians hold free, open, and fair elections.

- GOI facilitates Task Force election assistance, registration of voters, movement of candidates and voting officials. Support for [nongovernmental organizations (NGOs)] involved in the election process.

- GOI reopens Palestinian Chamber of Commerce and other closed Palestinian institutions in East Jerusalem based on a commitment that these institutions operate strictly in accordance with prior agreements between the parties.

Humanitarian Response

- Israel takes measures to improve the humanitarian situation. Israel and Palestinians implement in full all recommendations of the Bertini report to improve humanitarian conditions, lifting curfews and easing restrictions on movement of persons and goods, and allowing full, safe, and unfettered access of international and humanitarian personnel.

- [The Ad Hoc Liaison Committee (AHLC)] reviews the humanitarian situation and prospects for economic development in the West Bank and Gaza and launches a major donor assistance effort, including to the reform effort.

- GOI and [the Palestinian Authority] continue revenue clearance process and transfer of funds, including arrears, in accordance with agreed, transparent monitoring mechanism.

Civil Society

■ Continued donor support, including increased funding through [private voluntary organizations (PVOs)]/NGOs, for people to people programs, private sector development, and civil society initiatives.

Settlements

■ GOI immediately dismantles settlement outposts erected since March 2001.

■ Consistent with the Mitchell Report, GOI freezes all settlement activity (including natural growth of settlements).

Phase II: Transition, June 2003–December 2003

In the second phase, efforts are focused on the option of creating an independent Palestinian state with provisional borders and attributes of sovereignty, based on the new constitution, as a way station to a permanent status settlement. As has been noted, this goal can be achieved when the Palestinian people have a leadership acting decisively against terror, willing and able to build a practicing democracy based on tolerance and liberty. With such a leadership, reformed civil institutions, and security structures, the Palestinians will have the active support of the Quartet and the broader international community in establishing an independent, viable state.

Progress into Phase II will be based upon the consensus judgment of the Quartet of whether conditions are appropriate to proceed, taking into account performance of both parties. Furthering and sustaining efforts to normalize Palestinian lives and build Palestinian institutions, Phase II starts after Palestinian elections and ends with possible creation of an independent Palestinian state with provisional borders in 2003. Its primary goals are continued comprehensive security performance and effective security cooperation, continued normalization of Palestinian life and institution-building, further building on and sustaining of the goals outlined in Phase I, ratification of a democratic Palestinian constitution, formal establishment of [the] office of prime minister, consolidation of political reform, and the creation of a Palestinian state with provisional borders.

- International Conference: Convened by the Quartet, in consultation with the parties, immediately after the successful conclusion of Palestinian elections, to support Palestinian economic recovery and launch a process, leading to establishment of an independent Palestinian state with provisional borders. Such a meeting would be inclusive, based on the goal of a comprehensive Middle East peace (including between Israel and Syria, and Israel and Lebanon), and based on the principles described in the preamble to this document.

- Arab states restore pre-intifada links to Israel (trade offices, etc.).

- Revival of multilateral engagement on issues including regional water resources, environment, economic development, refugees, and arms control issues.

- New constitution for democratic, independent Palestinian state is finalized and approved by appropriate Palestinian institutions. Further elections, if required, should follow approval of the new constitution.

- Empowered reform cabinet with office of prime minister formally established, consistent with draft constitution.

- Continued comprehensive security performance, including effective security cooperation on the bases laid out in Phase I.

- Creation of an independent Palestinian state with provisional borders through a process of Israeli-Palestinian engagement, launched by the international conference. As part of this process, implementation of prior agreements, to enhance maximum territorial contiguity, including further action on settlements in conjunction with establishment of a Palestinian state with provisional borders.

- Enhanced international role in monitoring transition, with the active, sustained, and operational support of the Quartet.

- Quartet members promote international recognition of Palestinian state, including possible UN membership.

Phase III: Permanent Status Agreement and End of the Israeli-Palestinian Conflict, 2004–2005

Progress into Phase III, based on consensus judgment of Quartet, and taking into account actions of both parties and Quartet monitoring. Phase III objectives are consolidation of reform and stabilization of Palestinian institutions, sustained, effective Palestinian security performance, and Israeli-Palestinian negotiations aimed at a permanent status agreement in 2005.

- Second International Conference: Convened by Quartet, in consultation with the parties, at beginning of 2004 to endorse agreement reached on an independent Palestinian state with provisional borders and formally to launch a process with the active, sustained, and operational support of the Quartet, leading to a final, permanent status resolution in 2005, including on borders, Jerusalem, refugees, settlements; and to support progress toward a comprehensive Middle East settlement between Israel and Lebanon and Israel and Syria, to be achieved as soon as possible.

- Continued comprehensive, effective progress on the reform agenda laid out by the Task Force in preparation for final status agreement.

- Continued sustained and effective security performance, and sustained, effective security cooperation on the bases laid out in Phase I.

- International efforts to facilitate reform and stabilize Palestinian institutions and the Palestinian economy, in preparation for final status agreement.

- Parties reach final and comprehensive permanent status agreement that ends the Israel-Palestinian conflict in 2005, through a settlement negotiated between the parties based on UNSCR 242, 338, and 1397, that ends the occupation that began in 1967, and includes an agreed, just, fair, and realistic solution to the refugee issue, and a negotiated resolution on the status of Jerusalem that takes into account the political and religious concerns of both sides, and protects the religious interests of Jews, Christians, and Muslims worldwide, and fulfills the vision of two states, Israel and sovereign, independent, democratic, and viable Palestine, living side by side in peace and security.

- Arab state acceptance of full normal relations with Israel and security for all the states of the region in the context of a comprehensive Arab-Israeli peace.

APPENDIX 4

Quartet Statement on the Peace Process, May 4, 2004

- UN Secretary-General Kofi Annan
- Foreign Minister Sergey Lavrov of the Russian Federation
- Foreign Minister Brian Cowen of Ireland in the Capacity of [European Union (EU)] Presidency
- Javier Solana, High Representative for Common Foreign and Security Policy of the EU
- European Commissioner for External Relations Chris Patten
- U.S. Secretary of State Colin L. Powell

Secretary-General Annan: ". . . Let me now read you what the Quartet has agreed:

"We reaffirm our commitment to our shared vision of two states living side by side in peace and security. One of those states will be Israel and the other a viable, democratic, sovereign, and contiguous Palestine.

"We call on both parties to take steps to fulfill their obligations under the Roadmap, as called for in Security Council Resolution 1515 and in our previous statements, and to meet the commitments they made at the Red Sea summits in Aqaba and Sharm al-Sheikh.

"In that context, we welcome the Israeli government's recent reaffirmation of its readiness to implement certain obligations under the Roadmap, including progress towards a freeze on settlement activity. We urge the Israeli government to implement these commitments and to fully meet its Roadmap obligations.

"We view the present situation in the Middle East with great concern. We condemn the continuing terror attacks on Israel and call on the Palestinian Authority to take immediate action against terrorist groups and individuals who plan and execute such attacks.

"While recognizing Israel's legitimate right to self-defense in the face of terrorist attacks against its citizens within the parameters of international

Source: Office of the Spokesman for the Secretary-General, United Nations

humanitarian law, we call on the government of Israel to exert maximum efforts to avoid civilian casualties.

"We also call on the government of Israel to take all possible steps now, consistent with Israel's legitimate security needs, to ease the humanitarian and economic plight of the Palestinian people, including increasing freedom of movement for people and groups, both within and from the West Bank and Gaza, removing checkpoints, and other steps to respect the dignity of the Palestinian people and improve their quality of life.

"The government of Israel should take no actions undermining trust, such as deportation, attacks on civilians, confiscation and/or demolition of Palestinian homes and property, and other measures specified in the Tenet work plan.

"The Quartet calls for renewed efforts to reach a comprehensive ceasefire, as a step towards dismantlement of terrorist capabilities and infrastructure and renewed progress towards peace through implementation of the Roadmap.

"We note the government of Israel's pledge that the barrier is a security rather than political barrier and should be temporary rather than permanent. We continue to note with great concern the actual and proposed route of the barrier, particularly as it results in the confiscation of Palestinian land, cuts off the movement of people and groups, and undermines Palestinians' trust in the Roadmap process by appearing to prejudge the final borders of the future Palestinian state.

"We took positive note of Prime Minister Sharon's announced intention to withdraw from all Gaza settlements and parts of the West Bank. This should provide a rare moment of opportunity in the search for peace in the Middle East. This initiative, which must lead to a full Israeli withdrawal and complete end of occupation in Gaza, can be a step towards achieving the two-state vision and could restart progress on the Roadmap.

"We further note that any unilateral initiatives of the government of Israel should be undertaken in a manner consistent with the Roadmap and with the two-state vision that underlies the Roadmap. We reaffirm President Bush's June 24, 2002 call for an end to the Israeli occupation that began in 1967, through a settlement negotiated between the parties.

"We also note that no party should take unilateral actions that seek to predetermine issues that can only be resolved through negotiation and agreement between the two parties. Any final settlements on issues such as borders and refugees must be mutually agreed to by Israelis and Palestinians based on Security Council Resolutions 242, 338, 1397, and 1515, the terms of reference of the Madrid Peace Process, previous agreements, and the initiative of Saudi Crown Prince Abdullah endorsed by the Beirut Arab League Summit. It must also be consistent with the Roadmap.

"We have agreed to undertake the following steps, with appropriate mechanisms established to monitor progress and performance by all sides.

"One, we will act on an urgent basis, in conjunction with the World Bank, the UN Special Coordinator (UNSCO) and the Ad Hoc Liaison Committee (AHLC), on the basis of a World Bank/UNSCO Rapid Assessment Study, to ensure that Palestinian humanitarian needs are met, Palestinian infrastructure is restored and developed, and economic activity is reinvigorated.

"Two, we are prepared to engage with a responsible and accountable Palestinian leadership committed to reform and security performance. The Quartet members will undertake to oversee and monitor progress on these fronts.

"Three, we will seek to ensure that arrangements are put in place to ensure security for Palestinians and Israelis, as well as freedom of movement and greater mobility and access for Palestinians. We underscore the need for agreed transparent arrangements with all sides on access, mobility, and safety for international organizations and for bilateral donors and their personnel.

"As Israel withdraws, custody of Israeli-built infrastructure and land evacuated by Israel should be transferred through an appropriate mechanism to a reorganized Palestinian Authority which, in coordination with representatives of the Palestinian civil society, the Quartet, and other representatives of the international community, will, as quickly as possible, determine equitable and transparent arrangements for the ultimate disposition of these areas.

"Four, effective security arrangements continue to be critical to any possibility of progress. Palestinian security services should be restructured and retrained consistent with the Roadmap to provide law and order and security to the Palestinians and to end terror attacks against Israel.

"Finally, we reaffirm our commitment to a just, comprehensive, and lasting settlement to the Arab-Israel conflict, based on Resolutions 242 and 338. We remind all parties of the need to take into account the long-term consequences of their actions and of their obligation to make rapid progress towards resumption of a political dialogue.

"An appropriate coordinating and oversight mechanism will be established under the Quartet's authority. We call on all states in the region to assert every effort to promote peace and to combat terrorism. . . ."

APPENDIX 5

G8 Statement: Gaza Withdrawal and the Road Ahead to Mideast Peace, June 10, 2004

The G8 welcomes the prospect of Israeli withdrawal from all Gaza settlements and from parts of the West Bank, following the Israeli Cabinet decision to endorse Prime Minister Sharon's initiative. The G8 looks forward to the implementation of this decision in 2005, recalling the Quartet statement of May 4 that it "welcomes and encourages such a step, which should provide a rare moment of opportunity in the search for peace in the Middle East." The G8 hopes that this disengagement initiative will stimulate progress towards peace in the region, the realization of Palestinian national aspirations, and the achievement of our common objective of two states, Israel and a viable, democratic, sovereign, and contiguous Palestine, living side by side in peace and security.

The G8 views the Quartet Roadmap as the way forward towards a comprehensive settlement and calls on all parties to abide by their obligations under the Roadmap. The G8 countries will join with others in the international community, led by the Quartet, to restore momentum on the Roadmap, to enhance humanitarian and economic conditions among the Palestinian people, and to build democratic, transparent, and accountable Palestinian institutions. We will also work to help ensure security and stability in Gaza and the areas of the West Bank from which Israel withdraws. We call on both sides to end all acts of violence.

In furtherance of these goals, the G8 calls upon the Quartet to meet in the region before the end of this month, engage with Israeli and Palestinian representatives, and set out its plans for taking forward in practical terms its declaration of May 4.

We support and commend all efforts, including those by Egypt, to resolve critical security issues relating to Gaza, and urge that this important work continue. We urge and support the rebuilding and refocusing of Palestinian security services in accordance with the Roadmap, so that they enforce the

Source: U.S. Department of State

rule of law, mount effective operations against all forms of terrorism, and report to an empowered Interior Minister and Prime Minister.

We believe the important work of the Local Aid Coordinating Committee to alleviate the humanitarian situation in Gaza and the West Bank must continue. We suggest that preparations should begin now for a meeting of the Ad Hoc Liaison Committee with the aim of revitalizing the Palestinian economy. We welcome and encourage international support for the World Bank–established Trust Fund as an accountable and transparent mechanism for receipt of international assistance. We also welcome plans of the Palestinian Authority to hold municipal elections beginning at the end of the summer, and believe that the Task Force on Palestinian Reform should meet soon to assist in preparations to assure that these and subsequent elections will be fair and transparent, and serve as the building block of democratic reform.

The G8 welcomes the international conference [of the UN Relief and Works Agency] in Geneva and supports close coordination between all groups involved in international assistance.

APPENDIX 6

Disengagement Plan Approved by the Israeli Cabinet, June 6, 2004

I. Background: Political and Security Implications

The State of Israel is committed to the peace process and aspires to reach an agreed resolution of the conflict based upon the vision of US President George Bush. The State of Israel believes that it must act to improve the current situation. The State of Israel has come to the conclusion that there is currently no reliable Palestinian partner with which it can make progress in a two-sided peace process. Accordingly, it has developed a plan of revised disengagement (hereinafter "the plan"), based on the following considerations:

A. The stalemate dictated by the current situation is harmful. In order to break out of this stalemate, the State of Israel is required to initiate moves not dependent on Palestinian cooperation.

B. The purpose of the plan is to lead to a better security, political, economic, and demographic situation.

C. In any future permanent status arrangement, there will be no Israeli towns and villages in the Gaza Strip. On the other hand, it is clear that in the West Bank, there are areas which will be part of the State of Israel, including major Israeli population centers, cities, towns and villages, security areas, and other places of special interest to Israel.

D. The State of Israel supports the efforts of the United States, operating alongside the international community, to promote the reform process, the construction of institutions, and the improvement of the economy and welfare of the Palestinian residents, in order that a new Palestinian leadership will emerge and prove itself capable of fulfilling its commitments under the Roadmap.

Source: Office of the Prime Minister, Israel

E. Relocation from the Gaza Strip and from an area in Northern Samaria should reduce friction with the Palestinian population.

F. The completion of the plan will serve to dispel the claims regarding Israel's responsibility for the Palestinians in the Gaza Strip.

G. The process set forth in the plan is without prejudice to the relevant agreements between the State of Israel and the Palestinians. Relevant arrangements shall continue to apply.

H. International support for this plan is widespread and important. This support is essential in order to bring the Palestinians to implement in practice their obligations to combat terrorism and effect reforms as required by the Roadmap, thus enabling the parties to return to the path of negotiation.

II. Main Elements

A. The process

1. The required preparatory work for the implementation of the plan will be carried out (including staff work to determine criteria, definitions, evaluations, and preparations for required legislation).

2. Immediately upon completion of the preparatory work, a discussion will be held by the Government in order to make a decision concerning the relocation of settlements, taking into consideration the circumstances prevailing at that time—whether or not to relocate, and which settlements. The towns and villages will be classified into four groups, as follows:

> Group A: Morag, Netzarim, Kfar Darom
> Group B: the villages of Northern Samaria (Ganim, Kadim, Sa-Nur, and Homesh).
> Group C: the towns and villages of Gush Katif
> Group D: the villages of the Northern Gaza Strip (Elei Sinai, Dugit, and Nissanit)

It is clarified that, following the completion of the aforementioned preparations, the Government will convene periodically in order to decide separately on the question of whether or not to relocate, with respect to each of the aforementioned groups.

3. The continuation of the aforementioned process is subject to the resolutions that the Government will pass, as mentioned above in Article 2, and will be implemented in accordance with the content of those resolutions.

The Gaza Strip

a. The State of Israel will evacuate the Gaza Strip, including all existing Israeli towns and villages, and will redeploy outside the Strip. This will not include military deployment in the area of the border between the Gaza Strip and Egypt ("the Philadelphia Route") as detailed below.

b. Upon completion of this process, there shall no longer be any permanent presence of Israeli security forces in the areas of Gaza Strip territory which have been evacuated.

The West Bank

a. The State of Israel will evacuate an area in Northern Samaria (Ganim, Kadim, Sa-Nur, and Homesh), and all military installations in this area, and will redeploy outside the vacated area.

b. Upon completion of this process, there shall no longer be any permanent presence of Israeli security forces in this area.

c. The move will enable territorial contiguity for Palestinians in the Northern Samaria area.

d. The State of Israel will assist, together with the international community, in improving the transportation infrastructure in the West Bank in order to facilitate the contiguity of Palestinian transportation.

e. The process will facilitate normal life and Palestinian economic and commercial activity in the West Bank.

The intention is to complete the planned relocation process by the end of 2005.

B. The security fence

The State of Israel will continue building the Security Fence, in accordance with the relevant decisions of the Government. The route will take into account humanitarian considerations.

III. Security Situation Following the Relocation

A. The Gaza Strip

1. The State of Israel will guard and monitor the external land perimeter of the Gaza Strip, will continue to maintain exclusive authority in Gaza air space, and will continue to exercise security activity in the sea off the coast of the Gaza Strip.

2. The Gaza Strip shall be demilitarized and shall be devoid of weaponry, the presence of which does not accord with the Israeli-Palestinian agreements.

3. The State of Israel reserves its fundamental right of self-defense, both preventive and reactive, including where necessary the use of force, in respect of threats emanating from the Gaza Strip.

B. The West Bank

1. Upon completion of the evacuation of the Northern Samaria area, no permanent Israeli military presence will remain in this area.

2. The State of Israel reserves its fundamental right of self-defense, both preventive and reactive, including where necessary the use of force, in respect of threats emanating from the Northern Samaria area.

3. In other areas of the West Bank, current security activity will continue. However, as circumstances require, the State of Israel will consider reducing such activity in Palestinian cities.

4. The State of Israel will work to reduce the number of internal checkpoints throughout the West Bank.

IV. Military Installations and Infrastructure in the Gaza Strip and Northern Samaria

In general, these will be dismantled and evacuated, with the exception of those which the State of Israel decides to transfer to another party.

V. Security Assistance to the Palestinians

The State of Israel agrees that by coordination with it, advice, assistance, and training will be provided to the Palestinian security forces for the implementation of their obligations to combat terrorism and maintain public order, by American, British, Egyptian, Jordanian, or other experts, as agreed therewith.

No foreign security presence may enter the Gaza Strip and/or the West Bank without being coordinated with and approved by the State of Israel.

VI. The Border Area between the Gaza Strip and Egypt (Philadelphia Route)

The State of Israel will continue to maintain a military presence along the border between the Gaza Strip and Egypt (Philadelphia Route). This presence is an essential security requirement. At certain locations, security considerations may require some widening of the area in which the military activity is conducted.

Subsequently, the evacuation of this area will be considered. Evacuation of the area will be dependent, inter alia, on the security situation and the extent of cooperation with Egypt in establishing a reliable alternative arrangement.

If and when conditions permit the evacuation of this area, the State of Israel will be willing to consider the possibility of the establishment of a seaport and airport in the Gaza Strip, in accordance with arrangements to be agreed with Israel.

VII. Real Estate Assets

In general, residential dwellings and sensitive structures, including synagogues, will not remain. The State of Israel will aspire to transfer other facilities, including industrial, commercial, and agricultural ones, to a third, international party which will put them to use for the benefit of the Palestinian population that is not involved in terror.

The area of the Erez industrial zone will be transferred to the responsibility of an agreed upon Palestinian or international party.

The State of Israel will explore, together with Egypt, the possibility of establishing a joint industrial zone on the border of the Gaza Strip, Egypt, and Israel.

VIII. Civil Infrastructure and Arrangements

Infrastructure relating to water, electricity, sewage, and telecommunications will remain in place.

In general, Israel will continue, for full price, to supply electricity, water, gas, and petrol to the Palestinians, in accordance with current arrangements.

Other existing arrangements, such as those relating to water and the electromagnetic sphere, shall remain in force.

IX. Activity of Civilian International Organizations

The State of Israel recognizes the great importance of the continued activity of international humanitarian organizations and others engaged in civil development, assisting the Palestinian population.

The State of Israel will coordinate with these organizations arrangements to facilitate their activities.

The State of Israel proposes that an international apparatus be established (along the lines of the [Ad Hoc Liaison Committee]), with the agreement of Israel and international elements which will work to develop the Palestinian economy.

X. Economic Arrangements

In general, the economic arrangements currently in operation between the State of Israel and the Palestinians shall remain in force. These arrangements include, inter alia:

1. The entry and exit of goods between the Gaza Strip, the West Bank, the State of Israel, and abroad.
2. The monetary regime.

3. Tax and customs envelope arrangements.
4. Postal and telecommunications arrangements.
5. The entry of workers into Israel, in accordance with the existing criteria.

In the longer term, and in line with Israel's interest in encouraging greater Palestinian economic independence, the State of Israel expects to reduce the number of Palestinian workers entering Israel, to the point that it ceases completely. The State of Israel supports the development of sources of employment in the Gaza Strip and in Palestinian areas of the West Bank, by international elements.

XI. International Passages

A. The international passage between the Gaza Strip and Egypt

1. The existing arrangements shall continue.
2. The State of Israel is interested in moving the passage to the "three borders" area south of its current location. This would need to be effected in coordination with the Government of Egypt. This move would enable the hours of operation of the passage to be extended.

B. The international passages between the West Bank and Jordan:

The existing arrangements shall continue.

XII. Erez Crossing Point

The Erez crossing point will be moved to a location within Israel in a time frame to be determined separately by the Government.

XIII. Conclusion

The goal is that implementation of the plan will lead to improving the situation and breaking the current deadlock. If and when there is evidence from the Palestinian side of its willingness, capability, and implementation in practice of the fight against terrorism, full cessation of terrorism and violence, and the institution of reform as required by the Road Map, it will be possible to return to the track of negotiation and dialogue.

Format of the Preparatory Work for the Revised Disengagement Plan

1. A process of relocation involves many significant personal repercussions for the relocated residents. In implementing the plan, the Government of Israel is obliged to consider the implications for the relocated residents, assist them, and ease the process for them as much as possible. The difficulties and sensitivities involved in the process must be born in mind by the Government and by those who implement the process.

2. The Government of Israel attributes great importance to conducting a dialogue with the population designated for relocation regarding various issues relating to the implementation of the plan—including with respect to relocation and compensation—and will act to conduct such a dialogue.

Establishing an Organizational Framework

3. An organizational framework will be established with the purpose of addressing and assisting in all matters related to the implementation of the plan.

4. The Ministerial Committee for National Security (The Security Cabinet) will accompany and direct the Revised Disengagement Plan, including acceleration of the construction of the Security Fence, with the exception of the decisions concerning relocation. The Security Cabinet will be responsible for the implementation of this Government Resolution.

5. A Steering Committee is hereby established that will be responsible for coordinating the issues pertaining to the Revised Disengagement Plan. The Steering Committee will report to the Security Cabinet on its activities and bring before it issues which require a decision by the political echelon. The Steering Committee will include the following members:

Head of the National Security Council—Chairman
Representatives of the Ministry of Defense, the [Israel Defense Forces (IDF)], and the Israel Police
Director General of the Prime Minister's Office
Director General of the Ministry of Finance
Director General of the Ministry of Justice

Director General of the Ministry of Foreign Affairs
Director General of the Ministry of Industry, Trade, and Labor
Director General of the Ministry of Agriculture and Rural
  Development
Director General of the Ministry of National Infrastructures
Director General of the Ministry of the Interior
Director General of the Ministry of Construction and Housing

6. A Committee on Relocation, Compensation, and Alternative Settlement is hereby established which will be charged with the task of preparing legislation regarding relocation and compensation, as well as details of the principles and indexes for compensation, including incentives, advance payments, and compensatory aspects of relocation alternatives in priority areas, in accordance with Government policy. The Committee's recommendations will be presented to the Security Cabinet and serve as a basis for the draft bill on this issue.

This committee will constitute the exclusive authorized body for the coordination and conducting of dialogue with the population designated for relocation and compensation, and with all other bodies related to the issue of compensation—until the completion of the legislation. The Committee will be able to establish professional sub-committees, as it deems necessary, for the sake of fulfilling its tasks. The committee will include the following members:

Director General of the Ministry of Justice—Chairman
Representative of the Ministry of Finance
Representative of the Ministry of Industry, Trade, and Labor
Representative of the Ministry of Agriculture and Rural Development
Representative of the Prime Minister's Office

7. The Jewish Agency for Israel, as a body involved in settlement, will act in accordance with instructions from the Steering Committee and in coordination with the Committee on Relocation, Compensation, and Alternative Settlement. The role of the Jewish Agency will be to carry out the activities required for alternative settlement, either agricultural or communal, for those among the relocated civilian population who so desire.

8. a. An Executive Administration is hereby established in the Prime Minister's Office which will be subordinate to the Steering Committee. Its task will be to implement this Government Resolution with regard to the relocation of civilians and compensation.

b. The Executive Administration will be authorized to grant advance payments to those eligible for compensation—which will be counted against the compensation to be owed to them—according to terms that will be determined by the Committee on Relocation, Compensation, and Alternative Settlement, and in accordance with the instructions and procedures established by the said Committee.

c. The Head of the Executive Administration will hold the rank of Ministry Director General.

9. All Government ministries and other governmental bodies will forward, without delay, all information required for the aforementioned organizational frameworks to fulfill their tasks.

Legislation

10. a. The Ministry of Justice will formulate and the Prime Minister will submit, as soon as possible, a draft bill to the Ministerial Committee for Legislation, which will include provisions regarding relocation and compensation for those eligible, as well as the authority necessary for this purpose.

b. Soon thereafter, the Government will submit the bill to the Knesset.

c. The IDF Military Commanders in the Areas will issue the Security Legislation necessary for the implementation of the Government's Resolutions.

Budget

11. a. Within one month of the adoption of this Resolution, the Director of the Budget Division of the Ministry of Finance, in coordination with the Director General of the Prime Minister's Office and the Director General of the Ministry of Justice, will allocate the required budget and other resources necessary for the Steering Committee, the Committee on Relocation, Compensation, and Alternative Settlement, the Executive Administration, and the Jewish Agency to carry out their activities.

b. The 2005 Budget and subsequent budgets will be adjusted periodically to conform with the process and Government Resolutions on this issue.

c. For the sake of commencing its activities, the Executive Administration will be allocated, in the first stage, 10 staff positions.

Transition Instructions

12. During the interim period from the date this Resolution is passed, the following instructions will apply to the towns, villages, and areas included in the plan (hereafter "the towns and villages"), for the purpose of making preparations on the one hand, while maintaining normal and continuous daily life on the other:

a. Municipal and communal activities related to the course of normal life and services to which residents are entitled will continue unaffected, including services provided by the regional council, as well as security, education, welfare, telecommunications, mail, public transportation, electricity, water, gas, petrol, health services, banks, and all other services customarily provided to towns and villages prior to this Resolution.

b. Government plans for construction and development that have yet to commence will not be advanced for implementation.

c. Nothing stated in this Resolution is intended to undermine Government Resolution no. 150, dated August 2, 1996, regarding other areas. The aforementioned Government Resolution no. 150 will also apply to towns and villages for the purpose of approval prior to planning and land allocation.

Exceptional Cases Committee

13. An Exceptional Cases Committee will be established which will be authorized to permit the implementation of any plan which was frozen, in accordance with the provisions above, and authorized to decide not to advance plans even if their implementation has already commenced, fol-

lowing an examination of each individual case, and in keeping with criteria that it shall establish.

The Exceptional Cases Committee will be headed by the Director General of the Prime Minister's Office, and will include the Directors General
of the Ministries of Finance and Justice.

Decisions of the Exceptional Cases Committee may be appealed to the
Security Cabinet, in any instance where they are brought before it by a
member of the Government.

Principles for Compensation

14. a. The date which determines the right for compensation is the date of
the adoption of this Government Resolution.

b. Those entitled to compensation will receive fair and suitable compensation, as will be set out in the law legislated for this purpose.

APPENDIX 7

Prime Minister Sharon's Knesset Address before the Disengagement Vote, October 25, 2004

"This is a fateful hour for Israel. We are on the threshold of a difficult decision the likes of which we have seldom faced, the significance of which for the future of our country in this region is consistent with the difficulty, pain, and dispute it arouses within us. You know that I do not say these things with a light heart to the representatives of the nation and to the entire nation watching and listening to every word uttered here in the Knesset today. This is a people who has courageously faced, and still faces, the burden and terror of the ongoing war, which has continued from generation to generation; in which, as in a relay race, fathers pass the guns to their sons; in which the boundary between the frontline and the home front has long been erased; in which schools and hotels, restaurants and marketplaces, cafes and buses have also become targets for cruel terror and premeditated murder.

"Today, this nation wants to know what decision this house will make at the end of this stormy discussion. What will we say to them, and what message will we convey to them? For me, this decision is unbearably difficult. During my years as a fighter and commander, as a politician, Member of Knesset, as a minister in Israel's governments, and as prime minister, I have never faced so difficult a decision.

"I know the implications and impact of the Knesset's decision on the lives of thousands of Israelis who have lived in the Gaza Strip for many years, who were sent there on behalf of the governments of Israel, and who built homes there, planted trees and grew flowers, and who gave birth to sons and daughters, who have not known any other home. I am well aware of the fact that I sent them and took part in this enterprise, and many of these people are my personal friends. I am well aware of their pain, rage, and despair. However, as much as I understand everything they are going through during these days and everything they will face as a result of

Source: Knesset, Israel

the necessary decision to be made in the Knesset today, I also believe in the necessity of taking the step of disengagement in these areas, with all the pain it entails, and I am determined to complete this mission. I am firmly convinced and truly believe that this disengagement will strengthen Israel's hold over territory which is essential to our existence, and will be welcomed and appreciated by those near and far, reduce animosity, break through boycotts and sieges, and advance us along the path of peace with the Palestinians and our other neighbors.

"I am accused of deceiving the people and the voters because I am taking steps which are in total opposition to past things I have said and deeds I have done. This is a false accusation. Both during the elections and as prime minister, I have repeatedly and publicly said that I support the establishment of a Palestinian state alongside the state of Israel. I have repeatedly and openly said that I am willing to make painful compromises in order to put an end to this ongoing and malignant conflict between those who struggle over this land, and that I would do my utmost in order to bring peace.

"And I wish, Mr. Chairman, to say that many years before, in 1988, in a meeting with Prime Minister Yitzhak Shamir and with the ministers of the Likud, I said there that I believe that if we do not want to be pushed back to the 1967 lines, the territory should be divided.

"As one who fought in all of Israel's wars, and learned from personal experience that without proper force, we do not have a chance of surviving in this region, which does not show mercy towards the weak, I have also learned from experience that the sword alone cannot decide this bitter dispute in this land.

"I have been told that the disengagement will be interpreted as a shameful withdrawal under pressure, and will increase the terror campaign, present Israel as weak, and will show our people as a nation unwilling to fight and to stand up for itself. I reject that statement outright. We have the strength to defend this country, and to strike at the enemy which seeks to destroy us.

"And there are those who tell me that, in exchange for a genuine signed peace agreement, they too would be willing to make these painful compromises. However, regrettably, we do not have a partner on the other side with whom to conduct genuine dialogue in order to achieve a peace agreement. Even prime ministers of Israel who declared their willingness to relinquish the maximum territory of our homeland were answered with fire and hostility. Recently, the chairman of the Palestinian Authority declared that "a million *shaheeds* will break through to Jerusalem." In the choice between a responsible and wise action in history, which may lead to painful compromise, and a "holy war" to destroy Israel, Yasser Arafat chose the latter—the path of blood, fire, and *shaheeds*. He seeks to turn a national conflict which can be terminated through mutual understanding into a religious war between Islam and Jews, and even to spill the blood of Jews who live far away.

"Israel has many hopes, and faces extreme dangers. The most prominent danger is Iran, which is making every effort to acquire nuclear weapons and ballistic missiles, and establishing an enormous terror network together with Syria in Lebanon. And I ask you: what are we doing and what are we struggling over in the face of these terrible dangers? Are we not capable of uniting to meet this threat? This is the true question.

"The disengagement plan does not replace negotiations and is not meant to permanently freeze the situation which will be created. It is an essential and necessary step in a situation which currently does not enable genuine negotiations for peace. However, everything remains open for a future agreement, which will hopefully be achieved when this murderous terror ends, and our neighbors will realize that they cannot triumph over us in this land.

"Mr. Chairman, with your permission, I will read several lines from a famous essay which was published in the midst of the Arab Revolt of 1936— and we must bear in mind that the Jewish community in Israel numbered less than 400,000. This essay by Moshe Beilinson was published in *Davar*, as I mentioned, during the murderous Arab Revolt of 1936 (and I quote):

> How much longer? People ask. How much longer? Until the strength of Israel in its land will condemn and defeat in advance any enemy attack; until the most enthusiastic and bold in any enemy camp will know there are no means to break the strength of Israel in its land, because the necessity of life is with it, and the truth of life is with it, and there is no other way but to accept it. This is the essence of this campaign.

I am convinced that everything we have done since then confirms these emphatic words.

"We have no desire to permanently rule over millions of Palestinians, who double their numbers every generation. Israel, which wishes to be an exemplary democracy, will not be able to bear such a reality over time. The disengagement plan presents the possibility of opening a gate to a different reality.

"Today, I wish to address our Arab neighbors. Already in our declaration of independence, in the midst of a cruel war, Israel, which was born in blood, extended its hand in peace to those who fought against it and sought to destroy it by force (and I quote): 'We appeal—in the very midst of the onslaught launched against us now for months—to the Arab inhabitants of the state of Israel to preserve peace and participate in the upbuilding of the State on the basis of full and equal citizenship and due representation in all its provisional and permanent institutions.'

"A long time has passed since then. This land and this region have known more wars, and have known all the wars between the wars, terror and the difficult counter-actions undertaken by Israel, with the sole purpose of defending the lives of its citizens. In this ongoing war, many among the civilian population, among the innocent, were killed. And tears met tears. I would like you to know that we did not seek to build our lives in this homeland on your ruins. Many years ago, Zeev Jabotinsky wrote in a poem his vision for partnership and peace among the peoples of this land (and I quote): 'There he will be saturated with plenty and joy, the son of the Arab, the son of Nazareth, and my son.'

"We were attacked and stood firm, with our backs to the sea. Many fell in the battle, and many lost their homes and fields and orchards, and became refugees. This is the way of war. However, war is not inevitable and predestined. Even today, we regret the loss of innocent lives in your midst. Our way is not one of intentional killing.

"Forty-eight years ago, on the eve of our independence day in 1956, against the background of the return of the bodies of ten terrorists who committed crimes in Israel, murderous acts in Israel, and who were delivered in wooden coffins to the Egyptians at a border crossing in the Gaza Strip, . . . the Hebrew poet Natan Alterman wrote the following:

> Arabia, enemy unknown to you, you will awake when you rise against me,
> My life serves as witness with my back against the wall and to my history
>   and my G-d,
> Enemy, the power of whose rage in the face of those who rise to destroy
>   him until the day
> Will be similar only to the force of his brotherhood in a fraternal covenant
>   between
> one nation and another.

This was during the time of the terrorist killings and our retaliatory raids.

"Members of Knesset, with your permission, I wish to end with a quotation from Prime Minister Menachem Begin, who at the end of December 1977 said on this podium (and I quote):

> Where does this irresponsible language come from, in addition to other things which were said? I once said, during an argument with people from Gush Emunim, that I love them today, and will continue to like them tomorrow. I told them: you are wonderful pioneers, builders of the land, settlers on barren soil, in rain and through winter, through all difficulties. However, you have one weakness—you have developed among yourselves a messianic complex. You must remember that there were days, before you were born or were only small children, when other people risked their lives day and night, worked and toiled, made sacrifices and performed their tasks without a hint of a messianic complex. And I call on you today, my good friends from Gush Emunim, to perform your tasks with no less modesty than your predecessors, on other days and nights. We do not require anyone to supervise the Kashrut of our commitment to the Land of Israel! We have dedicated our lives to the Land of Israel and to the struggle for its liberation, and will continue to do so.

I call on the people of Israel to unite at this decisive hour. We must find a common denominator for some form of 'necessary unity' which will enable us to cope with these fateful days with understanding, and through our common destiny, and which will allow us to construct a dam against brotherly hatred which pushes many over the edge. We have already paid an unbearably high price for murderous fanaticism. We must find the root which brings us all together, and must carry out our actions with the wisdom and responsibility which allow us to lead our lives here as a mature and experienced nation. I call on you to support me at this decisive time."

APPENDIX 8

Exchange of Letters between Prime Minister Sharon and President Bush, April 2004

Letter from Prime Minister Sharon to President Bush

Dear Mr. President,

The vision that you articulated in your 24 June 2002 address constitutes one of the most significant contributions toward ensuring a bright future for the Middle East. Accordingly, the State of Israel has accepted the Roadmap, as adopted by our government. For the first time, a practical and just formula was presented for the achievement of peace, opening a genuine window of opportunity for progress toward a settlement between Israel and the Palestinians, involving two states living side by side in peace and security.

This formula sets forth the correct sequence and principles for the attainment of peace. Its full implementation represents the sole means to make genuine progress. As you have stated, a Palestinian state will never be created by terror, and Palestinians must engage in a sustained fight against the terrorists and dismantle their infrastructure. Moreover, there must be serious efforts to institute true reform and real democracy and liberty, including new leaders not compromised by terror. We are committed to this formula as the only avenue through which an agreement can be reached. We believe that this formula is the only viable one.

The Palestinian Authority under its current leadership has taken no action to meet its responsibilities under the Roadmap. Terror has not ceased, reform of the Palestinian security services has not been undertaken, and real institutional reforms have not taken place. The State of Israel continues to pay the heavy cost of constant terror. Israel must preserve its capability to protect itself and deter its enemies, and we thus retain our right to defend ourselves against terrorism and to take actions against terrorist organizations.

Having reached the conclusion that, for the time being, there exists no Palestinian partner with whom to advance peacefully toward a settlement,

Sources: White House; Ministry of Foreign Affairs, Israel

and since the current impasse is unhelpful to the achievement of our shared goals, I have decided to initiate a process of gradual disengagement with the hope of reducing friction between Israelis and Palestinians. The Disengagement Plan is designed to improve security for Israel and stabilize our political and economic situation. It will enable us to deploy our forces more effectively until such time that conditions in the Palestinian Authority allow for the full implementation of the Roadmap to resume.

I attach, for your review, the main principles of the Disengagement Plan. This initiative, which we are not undertaking under the Roadmap, represents an independent Israeli plan, yet is not inconsistent with the Roadmap. According to this plan, the State of Israel intends to relocate military installations and all Israeli villages and towns in the Gaza Strip, as well as other military installations and a small number of villages in Samaria.

In this context, we also plan to accelerate construction of the security fence, whose completion is essential in order to ensure the security of the citizens of Israel. The fence is a security rather than political barrier, temporary rather than permanent, and therefore will not prejudice any final status issues, including final borders. The route of the fence, as approved by our government's decisions, will take into account, consistent with security needs, its impact on Palestinians not engaged in terrorist activities.

Upon my return from Washington, I expect to submit this plan for the approval of the cabinet and the Knesset, and I firmly believe that it will win such approval.

The Disengagement Plan will create a new and better reality for the State of Israel, enhance its security and economy, and strengthen the fortitude of its people. In this context, I believe it is important to bring new opportunities to the Negev and the Galilee. Additionally, the plan will entail a series of measures with the inherent potential to improve the lot of the Palestinian Authority, providing that it demonstrates the wisdom to take advantage of this opportunity. The execution of the Disengagement Plan holds the prospect of stimulating positive changes within the Palestinian Authority that might create the necessary conditions for the resumption of direct negotiations.

We view the achievement of a settlement between Israel and the Palestinians as our central focus and are committed to realizing this objective. Progress toward this goal must be anchored exclusively in the Roadmap, and we will oppose any other plan.

In this regard, we are fully aware of the responsibilities facing the State of Israel. These include limitations on the growth of settlements; removal of unauthorized outposts; and steps to increase, to the extent permitted by security needs, freedom of movement for Palestinians not engaged in terrorism. Under separate cover we are sending to you a full description of the steps the State of Israel is taking to meet all its responsibilities.

The government of Israel supports the United States' efforts to reform the Palestinian security services to meet their Roadmap obligations to fight terror. Israel also supports the Americans' efforts, working with the international community, to promote the reform process, build institutions, and improve the economy of the Palestinian Authority, and to enhance the welfare of its people, in the hope that a new Palestinian leadership will prove able to fulfill its obligations under the Roadmap.

I want to again express my appreciation for your courageous leadership in the war against global terror, your important initiative to revitalize the Middle East as a more fitting home for its people, and, primarily, your personal friendship and profound support for the State of Israel.

Sincerely,
Ariel Sharon

Letter from President Bush to Prime Minister Sharon

Dear Mr. Prime Minister,

Thank you for your letter setting out your disengagement plan.

The United States remains hopeful and determined to find a way forward toward a resolution of the Israeli-Palestinian dispute. I remain committed to my June 24, 2002 vision of two states living side by side in peace and security as the key to peace, and to the road map as the route to get there.

We welcome the disengagement plan you have prepared, under which Israel would withdraw certain military installations and all settlements from Gaza, and withdraw certain military installations and settlements in the West Bank. These steps described in the plan will mark real progress toward realizing my June 24, 2002 vision, and make a real contribution towards peace. We also understand that, in this context, Israel believes it is important to bring new opportunities to the Negev and the Galilee. We are hopeful that steps pursuant to this plan, consistent with my vision, will remind all states and parties of their own obligations under the road map. The United States appreciates the risks such an undertaking represents. I therefore want to reassure you on several points.

First, the United States remains committed to my vision and to its implementation as described in the road map. The United States will do its utmost to prevent any attempt by anyone to impose any other plan. Under the road map, Palestinians must undertake an immediate cessation of armed activity and all acts of violence against Israelis anywhere, and all official Palestinian institutions must end incitement against Israel. The Palestinian leadership must act decisively against terror, including sustained, targeted, and effective operations to stop terrorism and dismantle terrorist capabilities and infrastructure. Palestinians must undertake a comprehensive and fundamental political reform that includes a strong parliamentary democracy and an empowered prime minister.

Second, there will be no security for Israelis or Palestinians until they and all states, in the region and beyond, join together to fight terrorism and dismantle terrorist organizations. The United States reiterates its steadfast commitment to Israel's security, including secure, defensible borders, and to preserve and strengthen Israel's capability to deter and defend itself, by itself, against any threat or possible combination of threats.

Third, Israel will retain its right to defend itself against terrorism, including to take actions against terrorist organizations. The United States will lead efforts, working together with Jordan, Egypt, and others in the international community, to build the capacity and will of Palestinian institutions to fight terrorism, dismantle terrorist organizations, and prevent the areas from which Israel has withdrawn from posing a threat that would have to be addressed by any other means. The United States understands that after Israel withdraws from Gaza and/or parts of the West Bank, and pending agreements on other arrangements, existing arrangements regarding control of airspace, territorial waters, and land passages of the West Bank and Gaza will continue. The United States is strongly committed to Israel's security and well-being as a Jewish state.

It seems clear that an agreed, just, fair, and realistic framework for a solution to the Palestinian refugee issue as part of any final status agreement will need to be found through the establishment of a Palestinian state, and the settling of Palestinian refugees there, rather than in Israel.

As part of a final peace settlement, Israel must have secure and recognized borders, which should emerge from negotiations between the parties in accordance with [UN Security Council] Resolutions 242 and 338. In light of new realities on the ground, including already existing major Israeli population centers, it is unrealistic to expect that the outcome of final status negotiations will be a full and complete return to the armistice lines of 1949, and all previous efforts to negotiate a two-state solution have reached the same conclusion. It is realistic to expect that any final status agreement will only be achieved on the basis of mutually agreed changes that reflect these realities.

I know that, as you state in your letter, you are aware that certain responsibilities face the state of Israel. Among these, your government has stated that the barrier being erected by Israel should be a security rather than political barrier, should be temporary rather than permanent, and therefore not prejudice any final status issues, including final borders, and its route should take into account, consistent with security needs, its impact on Palestinians not engaged in terrorist activities.

As you know, the United States supports the establishment of a Palestinian state that is viable, contiguous, sovereign, and independent, so that the Palestinian people can build their own future in accordance with my vision set forth in June 2002 and with the path set forth in the road map. The United States will join with others in the international community to foster the development of democratic political institutions and new leadership committed to those institutions, the reconstruction of civic institutions, the growth of a free and prosperous economy, and the building of capable security institutions dedicated to maintaining law and order and dismantling terrorist organizations.

A peace settlement negotiated between Israelis and Palestinians would be a great boon not only to those peoples but to the peoples of the entire region. Accordingly, the United States believes that all states in the region have special responsibilities: to support the building of the institutions of a Palestinian state; to fight terrorism, and cut off all forms of assistance to individuals and groups engaged in terrorism; and to begin now to move toward more normal relations with the state of Israel. These actions would be true contributions to building peace in the region.

Mr. Prime Minister, you have described a bold and historic initiative that can make an important contribution to peace. I commend your efforts and your courageous decision, which I support. As a close friend and ally, the United States intends to work closely with you to help make it a success.

Sincerely,
George W. Bush

Letter from Sharon Aide Dov Weisglass to National Security Advisor Condoleezza Rice, April 18, 2004

Dear Dr. Rice,

On behalf of the Prime Minister of the State of Israel, Mr. Ariel Sharon, I wish to reconfirm the following understanding, which had been reached between us:

1. Restrictions on settlement growth: within the agreed principles of settlement activities, an effort will be made in the next few days to have a better definition of the construction line of settlements in Judea and Samaria. An Israeli team, in conjunction with Ambassador Kurtzer, will review aerial photos of settlements and will jointly define the construction line of each of the settlements.

2. Removal of unauthorized outposts: the Prime Minister and the Minister of Defense, jointly, will prepare a list of unauthorized outposts with indicative dates of their removal; the Israel Defense Forces and/or the Israel Police will take continuous action to remove those outposts in the targeted dates. The said list will be presented to Ambassador Kurtzer within 30 days.

3. Mobility restrictions in Judea and Samaria: the Minister of Defense will provide Ambassador Kurtzer with a map indicating roadblocks and other transportational barriers posed across Judea and Samaria. A list of barriers already removed and a timetable for further removals will be included in this list. Needless to say, the matter of the existence of transportational barriers fully depends on the current security situation and might be changed accordingly.

4. Legal attachments of Palestinian revenues: the matter is pending in various courts of law in Israel, awaiting judicial decisions. We will urge the State Attorney's office to take any possible legal measure to expedite the rendering of those decisions.

5. The Government of Israel extends to the Government of the United States the following assurances:

   a. The Israeli government remains committed to the two-state solution—Israel and Palestine living side by side in peace and security—as the key to peace in the Middle East.

b. The Israeli government remains committed to the Roadmap as the only route to achieving the two-state solution.

c. The Israeli government believes that its disengagement plan and related steps on the West Bank concerning settlement growth, unauthorized outposts, and easing of restrictions on the movement of Palestinians not engaged in terror are consistent with the Roadmap and, in many cases, are steps actually called for in certain phases of the Roadmap.

d. The Israeli government believes that further steps by it, even if consistent with the Roadmap, cannot be taken absent the emergence of a Palestinian partner committed to peace, democratic reform, and the fight against terror.

e. Once such a Palestinian partner emerges, the Israeli government will perform its obligations, as called for in the Roadmap, as part of the performance-based plan set out in the Roadmap for reaching a negotiated final status agreement.

f. The Israeli government remains committed to the negotiation between the parties of a final status resolution of all outstanding issues.

g. The government of Israel supports the United States' efforts to reform the Palestinian security services to meet their Roadmap obligations to fight terror. Israel also supports the American efforts, working with the international community, to promote the reform process, build institutions, and improve the economy of the Palestinian Authority and to enhance the welfare of its people, in the hope that a new Palestinian leadership will prove able to fulfill its obligations under the Roadmap. The Israeli government will take all reasonable actions requested by these parties to facilitate these efforts.

h. As the Government of Israel has stated, the barrier being erected by Israel should be a security rather than a political barrier, should be temporary rather than permanent, and therefore not prejudice any final status issues, including final borders, and its route should take into account, consistent with security needs, its impact on Palestinians not engaged in terrorist activities.

Sincerely,
Dov Weisglass
Chief of the Prime Minister's Bureau

APPENDIX 9

Excerpts from Joint Bush-Sharon Press Conference, White House, April 14, 2004

President George W. Bush: ". . . Israel plans to remove certain military installations and all settlements from Gaza and certain military installations and settlements from the West Bank. These are historic and courageous actions. If all parties choose to embrace this moment they can open the door to progress and put an end to one of the world's longest-running conflicts. Success will require the active efforts of many nations. Two days ago I held important discussions with President Mubarak of Egypt, and I will soon meet with King Abdullah of Jordan. We're consulting closely with other key leaders in the region, in Europe and with our Quartet partners: the EU, Russia, and the United Nations. These steps can open the door to progress toward a peaceful, democratic, viable Palestinian state. Working together we can help build democratic Palestinian institutions as well as strong capabilities dedicated to fighting terror so that the Palestinian people can meet their obligations under the Roadmap on the path to peace. This opportunity holds great promise for the Palestinian people to build a modern economy that will lift millions out of poverty, create the institutions and habits of liberty, and renounce the terror and violence that impede their aspirations and take a terrible toll on innocent life.

"The Palestinian people must insist on change and on a leadership that is committed to reform and progress and peace. We will help, but the most difficult work is theirs. The United States is strongly committed, and I am strongly committed, to the security of Israel as a vibrant Jewish state. I reiterate our steadfast commitment to Israel's security and to preserving and strengthening Israel's self-defense capability, including its right to defend itself against terror. The barrier being erected by Israel as a part of that security effort should, as your government has stated, be a security rather than political barrier. It should be temporary rather than permanent, and therefore not prejudice any final status issues, including final borders. And

Source: White House

this route should take into account, consistent with security needs, its impact on Palestinians not engaged in terrorist activities. In an exchange of letters today and in a statement I will release later today, I'm repeating to the prime minister my commitment to Israel's security. The United States will not prejudice the outcome of final status negotiations and matters for the parties. But the realities on the ground and in the region have changed greatly over the last several decades, and any final settlement must take into account those realities and be agreeable to the parties.

"The goal of two independent states has repeatedly been recognized in international resolutions and agreements, and it remains a key to resolving this conflict. The United States is strongly committed to Israel's security and well-being as a Jewish state. It seems clear that an agreed, just, fair, and realistic framework for a solution to the Palestinian refugee issue as part of any final status agreement will need to be found through the establishment of a Palestinian state and the settling of Palestinian refugees there rather than Israel. As part of a final peace settlement, Israel must have secure and recognized borders which should emerge from negotiations between the parties in accordance with UN Security Council Resolutions 242 and 338. In light of new realities on the ground, including already existing major Israeli population centers, it is unrealistic to expect that the outcome of final status negotiations will be a full and complete return to the armistice lines of 1949, and all previous efforts to negotiate a two-state solution have reached the same conclusion. It is realistic to expect that any final status agreement will only be achieved on the basis of mutually agreed changes that reflect these realities. I commend Prime Minister Sharon for his bold and courageous decision to withdraw from Gaza and parts of the West Bank. I call on the Palestinians and their Arab neighbors to match that boldness and that courage. All of us must show the wisdom and the will to bring lasting peace to that region. Mr. Prime Minister, welcome to the White House."

Prime Minister Ariel Sharon: ". . . I want to thank you, Mr. President, for your warm welcome and your strong support and friendship for the state of Israel. I came to you from a peace-seeking country. Despite the repeated terror attacks against us, the people of Israel continue to wish for the achievement of a viable peace in accordance with our Jewish tradition, as outlined by Israel's prophets. Our people desire to be known for its achievement in the fields of culture, science, and technology, rather than in the battlefield. We are committed to make any effort to develop our country and society for our own benefit and for the benefit of the peoples of the region. In our meeting today, I presented to you the outlines of my disengagement plan. It will improve Israel's security and economy, and reduce friction and tension between Israelis and Palestinians. My plan will create a new and better reality for the state of Israel. And it also has the potential to create the right conditions to resume negotiations between Israel and the Palestinians.

"I was encouraged by your positive response and your support for my plan. In that context, you handed me a letter that includes very important statements regarding Israel's security and its well-being as a Jewish state. You have proven, Mr. President, your ongoing, deep, and sincere friendship for the state of Israel and to the Jewish people. I believe that my plan can be an important contribution to advancing your vision, which is the only viable way to achieve peace and security in the Middle East. I wish to end with a personal note. I myself have been fighting terror for many years, and understand the threats and cost of terrorism. In all these years, I have never met a leader as committed as you are, Mr. President, to the struggle for freedom and the need to confront terrorism wherever it exists. I want to express my appreciation to you for your courageous leadership in the war against global terror, and your commitment and vision to bring peace to the Middle East."

APPENDIX 10

Mahmoud Abbas Interview in *al-Sharq al-Awsat*, December 14, 2004

[Palestine Liberation Organization (PLO)] Executive Committee Chairman Abu Mazen [Mahmoud Abbas] has underlined the need to control and unite the Palestinian security organs and pointed to his agreement with the Palestinian factions to end the chaos of arms, saying the results would appear in the coming few weeks. He also underlined in an interview with *al-Sharq al-Awsat* his insistence on rejecting the militarization of the intifada and said, "An opinion is of no value if it remains an opinion. The opinion must be applied, and one of these applications is distancing the intifada from the weapons." He then noted that there was talk about Hamas and Islamic Jihad joining the PLO. Following is the text of the interview:

Nasser Qadih: There were fears of security chaos from the first moments after the death of President Yasser Arafat, especially what happened in Gaza when you were receiving condolences there. Where does the effort to control the security organs stand?

Mahmoud Abbas: Frankly, the Palestinian organs need to be controlled and brought together. There is security indiscipline. We were demanding and seeking to unite the security organs, and what happened in the condolences tent was the result of chaos, tension, and the charged atmosphere. It was also an opportunity to control the situation, and we have started to do so through our dialogues which have been split into two parts; the first deals with the security organs and the process of controlling them, and the second concerns the Palestinian organizations agreeing with them on ending these manifestations and the chaos of arms. We are hoping to reach positive results in the next few weeks.

Qadih: You had a clear opinion about the militarization of the intifada. Has the opinion remained just that or have you taken alternative steps?

Abbas: An opinion is of no value if it remains an opinion. The opinion must be applied, and one of these applications is distancing the intifada from the weapons. The intifada is a legitimate right for the people to express their rejection of the occupation through popular and social means, and this is what happened in the first intifada in the 1980s. The Palestinian people cannot be prevented from carrying out such activities that express their view. The use of weapons was harmful and it should be stopped through reaching tranquility among the ranks of the Palestinian people.

Qadih: How do you view reports of the possibility of Hamas and Islamic Jihad joining the PLO?

Abbas: Yes, there is talk under the slogan of Palestinian participation and also the presence of all in one assembly so that each person and each organization can play his role as they should. There is also talk about a unified leadership, how it ought to be within the PLO framework and how it can carry out its work. . . . There is also talk on their part about participating in the legislative elections so that they can be part of the Palestinian society's political fabric.

Qadih: You indicated in your letter of resignation as prime minister that there was a Palestinian group that did not want collective action. Will this group work with you in the coming stage?

Abbas: When we talk about democracy, there must be different decisions, decisions that sometimes may cause disagreement, . . . and this is healthy, permitted, and encouraged.

Qadih: Is this group still inside the leadership now?

Abbas: The leadership is now behind one man in the Fatah movement and in the PLO and marching side by side, believing in the future and the institutions. We hope that this is the procedure for future action.

Qadih: What do you say after Marwan al-Barghouti's official withdrawal from the elections?

Abbas: Brother al-Barghouti has the right to be a candidate and to withdraw. There is no pressure on him from anyone.

Qadih: Have you reached agreement on a specific mechanism for backing the peace process in your meetings with the Hamas and Jihad leaders in Palestine and Syria?

Abbas: It cannot be said that we agreed, but we discussed and raised all the issues. Nothing was left outside the framework of discussion. We have not reached anything so far but hope to agree in the future.

Qadih: What about the Syrian officials' help in this?

Abbas: I believe that the Syrian officials are willing to do so without being asked. There is no need for us to ask when we sense there is a willingness.

Qadih: Are there dialogues on the sidelines with the Israelis?

Abbas: If you mean negotiations, the answer is no. There are none, but there are constant dialogues and contacts about daily issues.

Qadih: There are reports of secret talks between [Palestinian foreign minister] Nabil Shaath and [Knesset minister] Omri Sharon in Britain. What was the outcome of these talks?

Abbas: I do not believe that this took place. As to negotiations, they might take place after the elections. There are no contacts at present.

Qadih: Why did you choose Syria, Lebanon, and Kuwait as the first countries to visit in your Arab and Gulf tour?

Abbas: There was no particular reason; it just happened as part of the program. We are confident of every step we take and also confident in our brothers who received us. It is not enough to have confidence in ourselves. We also have confidence in our brothers, that they will receive us when we visit.

Qadih: What about the Palestinian Islamic movements that are in Syria. Has the cessation of their activities been discussed?

Abbas: We talked to the Palestinian organizations that are present in Damascus, Hamas, Jihad, the Popular Front [for the Liberation of Palestine], and the Democratic Front [for the Liberation of Palestine], and held dialogues with them.

Qadih: Was a specific mechanism agreed on with them?

Abbas: The dialogue between them and us continues.

Qadih: Where do you believe it will lead?

Abbas: It will lead to an agreement.

Qadih: An agreement to cease their activities?

Abbas: It will lead to an agreement according to what all of us want. We now want a chance to work for the future and we are hoping to reach this agreement.

APPENDIX 11

Mahmoud Abbas Interview with al-Jazeera, January 7, 2005

Walid al-Umari: You were brave enough to call for an end to the chaos of arms, the militarization of the intifada, and the firing of rockets on Israel. Did you do so following contacts with the other Palestinian factions? Is this the policy you will adopt after your election?

Mahmoud Abbas: We have experience in this regard. This experience dates back to the time when I was [the] prime minister. That was my slogan when I presented my statement to the Legislative Council. I spoke about the chaos of arms, the militarization of the intifada, and other issues. I said this because we must put our house in order. I continued to adopt this policy. I say this very frankly to the organizations. On the basis of this, we observed a truce for fifty-two days last year. My dialogue with all organizations is based on this principle. What I say to the media, what I say behind closed doors, and what I say to the Palestinian, Arab, and international parties is exactly the same in style, language, and theme.

Al-Umari: When you were prime minister you reached a fifty-two-day truce with all Palestinian factions, but Israel did not respect the truce and continued its operations. That led to the deterioration of the situation. What makes you certain that such a truce will hold after the elections?

Abbas: We as Palestinians must adopt this policy and must put our Palestinian house in order. We will then address Israel and the world. If Israel wants to abide by this and choose the method of negotiations, then it is welcome. If not, this will be its own affair and the world—the Israeli people and the international community, particularly the Quartet Committee and the United States—will say its word about this. We cannot build our policy on what Israel might do. Nobody can tell what is on the mind of the

Source: Walid al-Umari, "Al-Jazirah Interviews Mahmud Abbas on Elections, Talks with Israel, Security," al-Jazeera Television, January 7, 2005, Foreign Broadcast Information Service (FBIS-NES-2005-0107), January 7, 2005.

Israeli government. We must do what we have to do and wait for the others to do what they have to do.

Al-Umari: You said you want the legitimate weapons to be one and united and, therefore, the chaos of arms must be ended. You also called for Palestinian political pluralism. Do you not fear that this might lead to collision with the Palestinian opposition factions?

Abbas: It will not lead to collision. This is proven by the fact that during the fifty-two-day truce there was no chaos of arms. There was only the one legitimate weapon. All abided by the truce. We have not clashed and nothing happened between us. I want to say that we will use the method of dialogue and only dialogue in order to reach this target. I have repeatedly said that shedding Palestinian blood with Palestinian hands is completely banned and we should not at all resort to it. I am sure that we will reach what we want through persuasion and dialogue because the other Palestinian parties also have a sense of responsibility. I think they can reach agreement on this issue.

Al-Umari: You have contacted several Palestinian organizations.

Abbas: Yes, I had contacts with all leaders in Gaza and Damascus. I explained my position to them and they explained theirs. I can frankly say that there was no disagreement on the substantial issues. We will continue this dialogue in order to finish discussing the elements of agreement before we can announce an agreement. In return, Israel must stop its attacks, killing, assassinations, and leveling of land. See what is taking place in Beit Hanun and Beit Lahiya—and I do not want to say in all of Palestine; I know the area from Jenin to Rafah. There is not a single green branch of tree in them. The Israelis bear a large share of responsibility.

Al-Umari: Your electoral platform consists of fourteen points. There are points related to the issue of refugees and these are reiterated in all platforms and are similar. What makes Mahmoud Abbas think he deserves a vote of confidence by the Palestinian people?

Abbas: I do not want to present myself in this way as the one who deserves or [is] most deserving and most capable. I am presenting myself as a Palestinian individual and struggler. We have been struggling since the 1950s. I present myself through my platform. I am known as a person who does not speak in two languages. This is how I thought of presenting myself. I said this frankly during all the meetings I held with the people in southern Gaza, the central region, Khan Yunis, Gaza, Beit Lahiya, Beit Hanun, and in all governorates and cities in the West Bank, in addition to Jerusalemites in Bir Nabala today. The talk is one and the language is one. This is how I present myself. If the Palestinian citizen is convinced of electing me, I will welcome this and will be happy and thankful for this confidence. I hope I will be worthy of this confidence if I succeed.

Al-Umari: You are chairman of the PLO and we are approaching the elections to elect a president for the West Bank and Gaza Strip. Some say you are using the PA's means and capabilities in your electoral campaign. Does the PLO chairman have the right to do so?

Abbas: I am using the same methods I have used since my return to the homeland in my capacity as PLO Executive Committee member and Fatah Central Committee member, and in my capacity as PLO Executive Committee secretary and then prime minister. I continued to be an Executive Committee secretary and then PLO chairman. The means I use are the same ones I have used over the past ten years.

Al-Umari: If elected president, what will your first decree be?

Abbas: The first decree will be asking brother Ahmed Qurei to tender his resignation and form a new government. The new government will prepare for the legislative elections in June this year, God willing. There will be a new electoral campaign and elections. There will also be a new government. This government will not continue, but Ahmed Qurei will be asked to form a new government as he deems fit pending the future elections. We do not know how these elections will end and who will win.

Al-Umari: Will the future government be formed as Ahmed Qurei or you deem fit?

Abbas: No, it will be his government and he is responsible for it before me and the Legislative Council. When I formed the government I was responsible before President Arafat and the Legislative Council. What applied to me applies to him.

Al-Umari: Are you optimistic about the next stage? You emphasized that you will embark on negotiations with the Israelis. Are you optimistic this time that these negotiations will be fruitful?

Abbas: As you said, I will embark on negotiations with the Israeli government. This will happen in the near future. It will certainly take place any time after the elections and the formation of the government. Our problem is with Israel. Therefore, our dialogue must also be with Israel. As for the issue of optimism and pessimism, I do not like to use these words. I can say that I am hopeful that we will reach something. If I had had no hope, I would not have been in this or any other position and I would not have sought to preside over the Authority. If I have no hope at all, why should I embark on such a hopeless adventure?

Al-Umari: How do you expect relations with the other factions and forces [to] be after the elections?

Abbas: We in the PLO and the factions have gotten used to differences, but these differences remain within the framework of the Palestinian house. We differ and then agree and then differ again and agree. This has been our situation since the establishment of the PLO. All enjoy a sense of responsibility, and this does not allow them to break away from what is customary in inter-Palestinian relations.

Al-Umari: One of the proposed issues on which work has started is unifying the security services in three bodies. There is also the issue of the (Israeli) pursuit of Palestinian fighters. What will the fate of the pursued ones be in the new era?

Abbas: These are two questions. The first is about the unification of the security services. The government has started work on this issue. We had the desire to do so before the Quartet Committee and the Roadmap called for it. Frankly speaking, we have many security bodies, and these sometimes conflict with one another and do not perform their duty in an acceptable manner. Therefore, they must be unified. The circumstances are now appropriate for the government to unify these services in three bodies. This is going on and I hope we will succeed in finishing this job.

Regarding the pursued ones, I had earlier reached agreement with the Israeli government about them when I was prime minister. The agreement called for absorbing them within the PA's frameworks and for guaranteeing their safety. This means they should not be pursued. The agreement was not finalized for several reasons. These include the failure of the truce, the fall of [the] government, and other reasons. This, however, is what I am seeking to do. This, too, is what I heard when I met with a large number of the al-Aqsa Martyrs Brigades members and other pursued brothers. I felt that they support the policy of my government, which has become known to them. At the same time, they have asked me to solve their problem in the manner I have explained. We must work for a solution, God willing, because they are young people whom we must protect and absorb. This is our duty toward them.

Al-Umari: Thank you, Mr. Mahmoud Abbas, PLO chairman and Fatah candidate for the Palestinian presidential elections.

APPENDIX 12

Summary of Revisions to the Disengagement Plan and Fence Route, February 20, 2005

- The Cabinet voted 17–5 to approve the Disengagement Plan and the evacuation of four groups of communities.

- The Cabinet approved the revised route for the security fence—20 ministers voted in favor, Minister Yisrael Katz voted against, Minister Natan Sharansky abstained.

Cabinet Communiqué
(Communicated by the Cabinet Secretariat)

At the weekly Cabinet meeting today (Sunday), 20 February 2005:

1. Prime Minister Ariel Sharon made the following remarks at the start of the meeting: "Today, the Cabinet will both discuss the evacuation of the communities included in the Disengagement Plan and make a decision. This will not be an easy day, nor will it be a happy day. The evacuation of communities from Gaza and northern Samaria is a very difficult step. It is difficult for the residents, for the citizens of Israel, for me, and I am certain that it is difficult for the members of the Cabinet. But this is a vital step for the future of the State of Israel." . . .

3. The Cabinet discussed the amended Disengagement Plan—the evacuation of communities and territories. Prime Minister Sharon summarized the discussion as follows:

"The Government's decision is important and vital for the State of Israel. From the moment that today's decision is made, all ministers and ministries are bound by it and must act to advance it. The decision that we will make today is that referred to in Article 22 of the law regarding the

Source: Ministry of Foreign Affairs, Israel

evacuation of each group of communities, which requires that the decision be made five months prior to the actual evacuation. It is in keeping with Minister Tzipi Livni's compromise, as it was approved by the Cabinet on 6 June 2004, regarding groups of communities; before the evacuation of each group, the Cabinet will convene in order to discuss and see if circumstances have changed, and decide accordingly.

"This is not an easy day. This is a tough decision, very tough for all of us. I know that there are ministers for whom today's vote is an especially harsh decision. These are among Israel's best people, who established regional enterprises under very harsh conditions and were steadfast for many years with uncommon heroism. I [asked] that ministers meet with them and I will invite them again. But the decision is a harsh one. There are times when leadership, determination and responsibility are called for, even if it doesn't seem popular, even if the decision isn't easy. We must remember that we are making this decision in order to advance the future of the State of Israel, and I very much appreciate the ministers' vote."

In continuation of decision #1996 of 6 June 2004, and in accordance with Article 22a of the Disengagement Implementation Law, the Cabinet decided, in regard to each group of communities, as follows:

a. Regarding the communities in the first group:
i. To evacuate the communities included in the first group as defined in the aforementioned Cabinet decision (Morag, Netzarim, and Kfar Darom);
ii. The Cabinet will reconvene shortly before the evacuation of the group, will discuss the then-existing circumstances, and will decide whether or not the circumstances are such that they will affect the evacuation.

b. Regarding the second group of communities:
i. To evacuate the communities included in the first group as defined in the aforementioned Cabinet decision (Northern Samaria communities: Ganim, Kadim, Sa-nur, and Homesh). . . .

c. Regarding the third group of communities:
i. To evacuate the communities included in the first group as defined in the aforementioned Cabinet decision (the communities in Gush Katif). . . .

d. Regarding the fourth group of communities:

  i. To evacuate the communities included in the first group as defined in the aforementioned Cabinet decision (the Northern Gaza Strip communities: Elei Sinai, Dugit, and Nisanit). . . .

e. In accordance with Article 22a of the 2005 Disengagement Plan Implementation Law, shortly after this decision is made, Prime Minister Ariel Sharon and Defense Minister Shaul Mofaz will, in an order or orders, determine the territories to be evacuated and the date of evacuation.

f. The discussions referred to above will be held from time to time, as will be determined for each group and as per the evacuation process.

4. The Cabinet discussed the revised route that has been proposed for the security fence and decided, in continuation of its previous relevant decisions and in the wake of substantive considerations stemming from the relevant High Court of Justice rulings on the continuation of work to build the fence, as follows:

"The Government views the continued construction of the security fence as important, as a means that has been proven effective in protecting the State of Israel and its residents, and in preventing the negative influence that a terrorist attack would be liable to have on the diplomatic process, while taking care to reduce, by as much as possible, its influence on Palestinians' daily lives, as per the High Court of Justice decision. In keeping with the foregoing:

a. The Cabinet approves the construction of the security fence for the prevention of terrorist attacks in accordance with the map appended to this decision. [Note: This map is included in David Makovsky and Anna Hartman, "Israel's Newly Approved Security Fence Route: Geography and Demography," *PeaceWatch* no. 495 (March 3, 2005); available online (www.washingtoninstitute.org/templateC05.php?CID=2268).] The map replaces and cancels the map that was appended to the 1 October 2003 Cabinet decision. The map appended to this decision is deposited with the Cabinet Secretariat.

b. The fence that is built in accordance with this decision, as well as the sections which have been already built, are a temporary security means for the prevention of terrorist attacks and do not express a diplomatic or any other border.

c. During the detailed planning, every effort will be made to reduce, by as much as possible, disturbances that are liable to be caused to Palestinians' daily lives as a result of the construction of the fence.

d. Local changes in the route of the fence or in its construction that stem from the overall planning for the route or from the need to reduce disturbances to Palestinians' proper daily lives will be submitted to the Diplomatic-Security Cabinet for approval.

e. Prime Minister Sharon, Defense Minister Mofaz, and Finance Minister Benjamin Netanyahu will agree on the scope of the budget necessary to implement this decision and the concomitant financing.

f. Sections in the route that have yet to receive legal approval are subject to legal approval (the Western Samaria area, the Maaleh Adumim area, and the Judean Desert). The construction of the security fence in accordance with previous decisions has proven its effectiveness in significantly reducing terrorist attacks. Completing the fence is vital to assuring the protection of the State of Israel and its residents. On 30 June 2004, the High Court of Justice handed down a decision that determined the parameters for building the barrier and emphasized the need to balance security needs with those of the Palestinian population. Following the decision, the IDF carried out staff work in cooperation with the Judea and Samaria Civil Administration and the Justice Ministry; all sections of the route were reconsidered in accordance with the parameters determined by the High Court of Justice. In the wake of this staff work, a revised route for the security fence, which will replace the route previously approved by the Cabinet, was submitted for Cabinet approval. Staff work on several sections of the route—in Western Samaria, in the vicinity of Maaleh Adumim, and in the Judean Desert—has yet to be completed; this will take all of the relevant security, civilian, and legal aspects into consideration.

Prime Minister Sharon and Defense Minister Mofaz Sign Orders Implementing Disengagement Plan
(Communicated by the Prime Minister's Media Adviser)

Prime Minister Ariel Sharon and Defense Minister Shaul Mofaz this evening (Sunday), 20 February 2005, signed an order implementing the

Disengagement Plan (Gaza Strip) and an order implementing the Disengagement Plan (Northern Samaria). The orders were signed in accordance with both the Disengagement Implementation Law and today's Cabinet decision, and determine that the evacuation day will be 20 July 2005.